OUT OF THE FRYING PAN

OUT OF THE FRYING PAN

THE STORY OF NEW CROSS SPEEDWAY

NORMAN JACOBS

First published 2008

STADIA is an imprint of
The History Press Ltd
Cirencester Road, Chalford,
Stroud, Gloucestershire, GL6 8PE
www.thehistorypress.co.uk

British Library Cataloguing in Publication Data.
A catalogue record for this book is available from the British Library.

ISBN 978 0 7524 4476 5

Typesetting and origination by The History Press Ltd.
Printed in Great Britain by Ashford Colour Press Ltd. Gosport, Hants.

Contents

Foreword

By Jim Blanchard

Growing up and living only a few streets away from New Cross Speedway I can vaguely remember being taken down there by my speedway-mad parents at the age of three or four years old. Sadly, shortly after they were to close, though I could still remember the smell of the Castrol R and the glitter of the wheel spokes being caught by the track lighting.

During the following years should a motorcycle obviously using the same Castrol R go by in the vicinity, my friends and I would assume that speedway had returned to New Cross. Of course we had our hopes dashed all the time, but we remained optimistic that speedway would once again return to the Frying Pan.

Then, when I reached the age of ten in 1959, the news came out that New Cross was going to reopen after all, for eight meetings and run by none other than Johnnie Hoskins and Tiger Hart. The expectation and excitement until that first meeting was hard to contain for me. My elder brother and his friend went to the stadium one day shortly before they opened and got themselves hired as track rakers.

I must have been there two hours early on the evening of the first meeting and got my viewing position on the pit wall. I just could not believe what I was seeing and hearing. It all came back to me straightaway that this sport will overdose all the senses. So that was it for me, every Wednesday for the next eight weeks or so perched on the pit wall. I was now seeing the best speedway riders in the world first hand. Riders like Peter Craven, Ronnie Moore, Barry Briggs and Ove Fundin. Peter quickly became my hero and personal favourite.

When the team was reformed the following year I got myself an after-school job working for ex-West Ham rider-turned-tuner of speedway engines, Ken Brett. He was now co-director of New Cross speedway. Through him and my little job of cleaning bikes, I really got to know some riders like Split Waterman and the South African Doug Davies. This would also lead me to traveling around the various tracks up and down the country helping out in the pits at the tender age of thirteen.

My biggest thrill was being in the pits for the World Championship final at Wembley in 1963, looking after the spare machine of finalist and former New Cross rider, Leo McAuliffe.

When New Cross Speedway finally closed its doors in 1963 it was the saddest day of my young life. It had provided excitement and fun for two generations of my family.

Jim Blanchard is a well-known speedway artist and runs several speedway tribute websites, including one dedicated to New Cross Speedway: www.newcrossspeedway.co.uk and the Speedway History Forum.

Introduction and Acknowledgments

The first speedway match I ever saw was on 11 May 1960, when I was twelve years old. Watching the stadium lights go down and then the floodlights pick out the four black-clad gladiators as they leapt away from the start, throwing their bikes into the first bend and wrestling with them for four laps of breathtaking excitement, hooked me immediately – and that was even before I smelt the Castrol R! The track where this conversion to a lifelong obsession took place was New Cross. I learnt afterwards that it was a generally held belief that racing at this track just off the Old Kent Road in South East London was the most exciting in speedway. Whereas most tracks had fairly decent-size straights, New Cross, because it was the smallest in the country, had hardly any and so the track was almost circular, which led to its nickname, the Frying Pan. This also ensured the extra excitement as the bikes seemed to be in a continual slide. I have long wanted to find out more about the history of the track that first got me into speedway and to write it up. Now, thanks to Rob Sharman at Stadia, I am able to do just that.

There are several people I would like to thank for helping to make this book possible. In particular, Peter Jackson, for his help with the statistics; Jim Blanchard for penning the foreword and other general support; John Hyam, the former editor of *Speedway Star*, for background information, as well as John Chaplin, Mike Kemp, Terry Stone and John Somerville for supplying a number of the photographs in the book.

I know there are many supporters out there who still mourn the passing of New Cross and I hope this book will bring back memories to them. To those who never got the opportunity to visit the most exciting track in speedway, *Out of the Frying Pan* will show them what they missed.

So, here goes:

1-2-3-4
WHO ARE WE FOR?
R–A–N–G–E–R–S
RANGERS!

one

How it Started

In 1926, Fred Mockford and Cecil Smith – two men operating as London Motor Sports Ltd – contacted the Trustees of Crystal Palace in South London with a proposal that they be allowed to mark out a mile-long circuit on the gravel pathways around the site and introduce motorcycle-path racing.

The two men complemented each other in their style and approach. Mockford was the sort of person who just bubbled over with enthusiasm for the sport. He was a born showman and it was said that 'Baloney' was his middle name. He would jump around at meetings and try to involve the crowd in everything that happened. He also fed stories to the Press, trying to get as much publicity as possible. Smith, on the other hand, was much more reserved and a dab hand at facts and figures. He was to become the announcer at Crystal Palace, then later at New Cross, and the crowd just knew that they could trust his calm, assured voice.

Responding to their approach, the Trustees agreed and path racing began.

Riders at these early meetings included Triss Sharp, Gus Kuhn, Joe Francis and one of the men who was to eventually be intimately involved in bringing speedway to this country from Australia, Lionel Wills.

Mockford and Smith were quick to recognise that this new sport of speedway would be a money spinner. It was the age of speed and watching these latter-day gladiators hurtling round the track at impossible angles, spraying flying cinders behind them, handlebars almost touching and seemingly on the verge of crashing at every corner, sent a thrill through even the most hardened spectators. It was new. It was electrifying. And everyone wanted to see it. And so, on 19 May 1928, Crystal Palace opened its doors to the new sport for the first time with a new track marked round the old football pitch.

The main event of that first day was a match between England and Australia, which took the form of three individual match races. The first heat pitted England's Lionel

Programme cover for the first meeting held at Crystal Palace on 19 May 1928.

Wills against Australia's Ron Johnson. Wills and Johnson continued to appear regularly at Crystal Palace during that first season along with path riders Joe Francis and Triss Sharp, and newcomers such as Roger Frogley and Harry Shepherd. When league speedway started the following year, Crystal Palace entered a team in the Southern League. The team, nicknamed the Glaziers for obvious reasons, took to the track for their first-ever league fixture away at White City on 3 May 1929. Their biggest triumph came in 1931 when they won the London Cup, beating the mighty Wembley in the final.

By the end of the 1933 season, visitor numbers to the Crystal Palace grounds were in general decline and the only two attractions that were still regularly pulling in large numbers were the path racing and the speedway. The trustees of the Palace felt they needed to make their money out of these and consequently proposed a dramatic increase in rent to something like £1,000 per week. This, combined with their refusal to sanction floodlights at the speedway track, forced the promoters to seriously consider their future at Sydenham and on 13 October, Messrs Mockford and Smith announced that they had completed negotiations to lay down a track at New Cross stadium, a few miles to the east, and would transfer their operation there at the start of the 1934 season.

After the last meeting on 14 October, therefore, it was a case of goodbye Crystal Palace, hello New Cross.

two

The 1930s

1934

New Cross opened its doors to the public for the first time on 18 April 1934. Faced with the necessity of constructing the circuit within the existing greyhound track, Mockford and Smith preferred to sacrifice length in favour of providing two very wide, sweeping bends joined by very short straights, making the track the shortest speedway in the country at 262 yards. The whole of the track was slightly banked, the most important feature of the banking being that instead of ceasing suddenly at the point where riders emerged on to the straight, it continued in such a way as to enable them to maintain a high speed without undue risk of crashing into the safety fence. For the first time in speedway, a tarmac foundation was used to eliminate the possibilities of any bumps arising. The greyhound tower was used in lieu of a steward's rostrum and, although this placed the official slightly in front of the finishing line, it was considered that this small disadvantage would be more than compensated for by the advantage of having an uninterrupted bird's-eye view of the whole track.

Mockford retained Johnson, Francis, Shepherd, Tom Farndon, Nobby Key, George Newton and Lew Lancaster from the 1933 Crystal Palace team and brought in juniors Les Gregory and Jack Dalton, along with Stan Greatrex and Roy Dook from the now-defunct Coventry.

Johnson, who remained as captain, had started his speedway career in Australia during 1926 and had played a large part with Mockford, Smith and Wills in introducing speedway to Crystal Palace in the first place. He was of slight build, weighing in at only 8st 6lbs. He was said to eat just one meal a day, a big breakfast, and if he got peckish during the day would down a quart of milk. He had the ideal temperament for speedway as he appeared to be totally nerveless. He was a great planner of races

An aerial view of New Cross stadium.

and worked out how he would ride each match before ever setting foot on the track. As a captain, he was one of the best and always more than ready to advise the team members on how to ride a particular track or help with the set-up on their bike.

The old Crystal Palace Supporters' Club now became the New Cross Supporters' Club. Membership cost one shilling and allowed cut-price admission to all enclosures. Even before the season started, membership applications were coming in at the rate of 600 per week and by the time of the official opening, numbers exceeded those of the old Crystal Palace club.

To keep some continuity the colours chosen for the new club were orange and black, the same as Crystal Palace, however, the emblem on the front of the body colours was changed from a star to a Maltese Cross, as a pun on the name New Cross.

Also, with the change of track it was felt a new nickname was required. In the programme for the opening night, Fred Mockford wrote:

WON 32-2[?]

Programme cover for the first meeting held at New Cross on 18 April 1934.

Of course we have not yet got a nickname for the team, but we naturally think you would soon find one. One of our supporters wrote into me the other day and suggested that as our track is between Canterbury Road and the Den (Millwall's Football Ground), a most suitable name would be 'The Lambs'; just think of the war-cry: 'Baa! Baa! Baa!'

The nickname The Lambs stuck for two seasons until a new name was chosen in 1936.

Crystal Palace had been noted for the excellence of its workshops and Mockford and Smith laid on the same set-up at their new track, with all the latest electrical equipment installed. The workshop was under the direction of Tommy Hall and Alf Cole, both ace motorcycle mechanics, with a team of mechanics under them.

The very first match ridden in New Cross colours was an away challenge at Wimbledon, which Wimbledon won 30-21. New Cross's first-ever heat winner was Joe Francis, who won Heat 3 beating the Dons' Claude Rye and Gus Kuhn.

The opening fixture at New Cross on 18 April attracted 15,000 spectators, all of whom went away happy with having seen a first-class match full of excitement, in good surroundings, with lighting to compare with any other stadium in the league and a good sound system. Even better for the home supporters was the fact that the match was won by New Cross, who beat West Ham 32-21, in their first league fixture, although the very first rider to cross the winning line at New Cross was the West Ham captain Tiger Stevenson. Tom Farndon firmly established himself as the favourite of the crowd by scoring a maximum, as well as setting the fastest time of the night – 63.0 seconds – which therefore became the first official track record. Farndon was already a big Crystal Palace favourite, having signed for them at the beginning of 1931 before going on to win the 1933 Star Riders' Championship, with his teammate, Johnson, in second place.

The first official away match saw the Lambs given the toughest possible task as it was at the runaway 1933 champions, Belle Vue, but thanks to Farndon, the newcomers gave the champions the shock of their lives as they ran them to within a single point, just losing out 26-25. He was easily the fastest rider on show, recording the two fastest times of the night, the fastest of which was two seconds quicker than that of the fastest Belle Vue rider.

Farndon scored another maximum in the next home match against Harringay, helping the Lambs to a 29-25 win. These two maximums at New Cross were the start of a phenomenal run at home for Farndon, as in his first six matches he won every race except two in which he fell and in the whole of the season, apart from falls or engine failures, he lost just four races to an opponent in 16 matches. Not only was he almost unbeatable but he was one of the most spectacular riders around, as he still kept to the old leg-trailing style and had the horrifying habit of flinging his machine so far over on the bends that in most races his knee was brushing the ground. He was then, by sheer physical strength, able to haul it upright again. He could ride inside or outside, hug the white line or scrape the fence, whichever seemed the best way at the time. His physical strength stemmed from the fact that he was a tee-total non-smoker and was always in the peak of condition. He was one of the few riders who could ride four laps and then come in without showing the slightest sign of the terrific exertion and strain he had undergone. To add to his appeal, Farndon was one of the most modest sportsmen around. He was said to be the only rider who would rather blame himself if he did not win a race rather than his machinery. And, as if that wasn't enough, he had all the good looks and charm of a Hollywood celebrity as well. Hero worship of this charismatic figure began to reach proportions that formerly only footballers and film stars could hope to aspire. The whole of South East London seemed in thrall to this man as he became the most popular speedway rider ever.

By the end of May, the Lambs were in third place in the league, behind Belle Vue and Wembley. A narrow defeat at West Ham, 26-27, showed how well the team were riding but did nothing to help the points situation. The several coach-loads of supporters who had gone to Custom House to cheer on their team were very upset by the narrow loss, as they felt they should have won following an incident in Heat 7. Greatrex and West Ham's Wal Morton crashed on their second lap and then on the final lap Johnson fell while in

The 1934 New Cross team. From left to right, back row: Harry Shepherd, Roy Dook, Stan Greatrex, George Newton. Front row: Joe Francis, Tom Farndon, Fred Mockford (promoter and manager), Ron Johnson (captain), Nobby Key.

the lead and Bluey Wilkinson had to lay his bike down. Greatrex, having remounted, was a long way behind but he came through to win. Wilkinson managed to paddle his bike along, pushing with his legs, but it took so long that he was excluded for exceeding the time limit and the red lights came on. Wilkinson, however, persevered and finished. The steward then changed his mind about the exclusion and awarded him two points. As it turned out, those two points made all the difference to the final result.

The fans' adulation of their hero, Tom Farndon, reached new heights at the next home meeting, the London Riders' Championship. Farndon won all his heats to qualify for the final where he met the Australian captain and newly crowned British Individual Match Race Champion, Vic Huxley, and Wembley's Ginger Lees in the final. Farndon shot straight into the lead as the tapes went up and went further and further in front, beating two of the best riders in world speedway by more than twenty lengths. The ovation that greeted Farndon's victory was said to be the longest and loudest ever accorded to a speedway rider in the history of the sport.

Following the London Riders' Championship, the New Cross management announced that they were going to lay down concrete terraces to make the standing accommodation more comfortable.

New Cross's next match was against the current champions and favourites for the 1934 title, Belle Vue. It turned out to be Belle Vue's second defeat of the season as the Lambs rode magnificently to win 31-21. New Cross's next victory, 30-24 over Wimbledon, put them second in the league and in their next two matches they ran

Harry 'Shep' Shepherd, a
Crystal Palace and New
Cross rider from 1928
until 1936.

riot over their opponents, winning 32-21 away at Plymouth and 39-14 at home to
Harringay. Farndon scored a maximum in each match.

Another honour came Farndon's way in the Test match at New Cross on 20 June,
when he lowered the track record to 61.4 seconds after an amazing second heat in
which he came from last to first, taking both Bluey Wilkinson and his own New Cross
captain, Ron Johnson, in the process. So solid was the New Cross team at this time, that
no fewer than four of them were chosen for their respective countries: Farndon, Key
and Francis for England and Johnson for Australia.

Buoyed by their good league form, the Lambs next took on West Ham in the
National Trophy second round. Thanks to the outstanding form of Johnson, who
scored an 18-point maximum, and Farndon, who suffered just one loss at the hands of
Tommy Croombs in the last heat, New Cross came away from Custom House with an
11-point advantage from the first leg, winning 59.5-48.5. The second leg, back at the
Old Kent Road, was a mere formality which turned into something of a rout as the
Lambs outrode the luckless Hammers to win 69-36 and 127.5-84.5 on aggregate. This

time it was Farndon's turn to score a maximum and Johnson's turn to lose out in one race. So one-sided was this match that the most exciting thing to happen all night was Dook's bike catching fire on returning to the pits after Heat 16.

Johnson and Farndon's good individual runs continued as Johnson won the Essex Open Championship at Lea Bridge – breaking the track record twice – and the Plymouth Open Championship, while Farndon broke the four-lap clutch-start records at West Ham and Wimbledon and the four-lap rolling-start records at Wembley and Plymouth – the latter record he broke by an incredible two seconds. Together they also won the National League Best Pairs' Trophy.

Midsummer 1934 was very dry and the shortage of water was badly affecting track preparation at New Cross, so the management sought and received permission to pump water from the nearby Surrey Canal. A three-inch iron pipe was laid for a distance of 395 yards from the canal to the edge of the track where a three-inch hose delivered the water at 100lbs pressure.

New Cross next met Harringay in the first round of the London Cup, scoring a 63-44 win away. Once again the damage was mainly done by Farndon and Johnson, with Nobby Key also contributing 13 points from five rides.

New Cross's ambition to at least take second place in the league, having given up on catching Belle Vue at the top, suffered a devastating blow on 19 July when they went down 33-20 at the home of their greatest rivals, Wembley.

The Lambs fared no better against Wembley in the National Trophy semi-final, losing 42-62 at home in the first leg. Johnson in particular was absolutely superb as he raced to an 18-point maximum, breaking the track record in the first heat with a time of 60.8, a time which not only broke the standing-start record but, amazingly, the rolling-start record as well. Johnson was in such stunning form that a hastily arranged two-lap-match race was slotted in the second half between him and Wembley's George Greenwood, in the hope that he would break that track record as well. He didn't disappoint.

Nobby Key was ruled out of the second leg at Wembley with an ankle injury and his place was taken by old Crystal Palace favourite, Triss Sharp. The final score was Wembley 67.5, New Cross 40.5, putting Wembley through to the final, 129.5-82.5.

The next home meeting, on 1 August, saw the return leg of the London Cup first round match against Harringay, which New Cross won 66-41 to go through to the semi-final 129-85 on aggregate. But it was the second leg of the British Individual Match Race Championship which everyone had really come to see that night. Earlier in the season, Vic Huxley had regained the title he had first won in 1931. There is no doubt that Huxley was the greatest name in the sport in its early years. He won the Star Riders' Championship in 1930 and was runner-up in 1929, 1931 and 1932. He was currently the Australian captain and had been an ever-present in the Test matches between England and Australia that had started in 1930. Even now, he was top of the National League averages, just ahead of Farndon. Huxley was still the rider everyone wanted to beat. Because of his sensational form throughout the season, the Control Board chose New Cross idol Farndon to be Huxley's next challenger. It was a real case of the old maestro versus the young pretender with the Press touting Huxley as favourite to win.

The first leg took place at Huxley's track, Wimbledon, on 30 July. Farndon won the toss, took the inside and shot away from Huxley, leaving him standing, to win the race by a convincing margin and beat the Wimbledon track record by three-fifths of a second. In the second race, Huxley managed to stay with Farndon as far as the first corner, but then Farndon went round Huxley as if the latter was standing still and again beat the Wimbledon captain by a big distance in an identical time to the first heat.

As news spread around South London of the challenger's performance, crowds flocked to New Cross to see the sport's new phenomenon take on the old master in the second leg and it was in front of a 30,0000-capacity crowd that Huxley won the toss and elected to go off the inside berth. This time it was Huxley who got away first and for almost two laps the Australian ace kept the young Briton at bay. But Farndon was not to be denied and, going round the fourth bend on the second lap, he pulled out all the stops and rode a magnificent corner, almost scraping the safety fence, passing Huxley as they came into the home straight. From then on, he gradually pulled away, winning the race by eight lengths. Although this had been an exciting enough race in itself, which had brought the crowd to its feet, it was when

Joe Francis commenced his association with Crystal Palace as a path rider in 1926 and continued with Mockford and Smith as a rider for Crystal Palace and New Cross until the outbreak of war in 1939.

the time was announced that there were loud gasps from the spectators. The time not only smashed the current four-lap rolling-start track record held by Eric Langton – by an astonishing 1.4 seconds – but it was the first time ever on any track in the country that the magic one-minute mark had been beaten as Farndon came home in 59.6 seconds. The second race was something of an anti-climax as Farndon led from start to finish, winning in 60.2 seconds, a time also well within the old track record. Later in the season, on 3 October, Farndon took the rolling-start track record down still further to an incredible 56.8 seconds.

Farndon had beaten the recognised master of world speedway easily in four straight runs, in each of which he had broken the existing track record on the two respective tracks. Farndon was now Star Riders' Champion, London Riders' Champion and British Individual Match Race Champion, the only rider in the history of the sport to hold all three major titles simultaneously. His film-star status was now confirmed and, in the eyes of all New Cross supporters, he could do no wrong.

Later in the season, Farndon successfully defended the championship twice more, once against Belle Vue's Max Grosskreutz and once against his own captain, Ron Johnson.

Back in league action, New Cross continued to annihilate the opposition, with wins over newcomers Walthamstow, 36-17, and Harringay, 39-14. Farndon scored a maximum in each and Johnson two paid maximums. There was a really solid look to the team now, which had settled down to Johnson, Key, Farndon, Greatrex, Francis and Newton, with Dook and Shepherd at reserve. Following further victories over West Ham and Birmingham, the Lambs produced the performance of the season, wiping out Plymouth, 42-9. Not only were New Cross invincible at home, but teams felt lucky if they managed to take 20 points from them.

In the two months between 6 August and 6 October, New Cross won nine out of the 11 matches they rode in home and away. Unfortunately, the two losses were against their main rivals, away at Wembley and Belle Vue, and they were enough to push the Lambs down to third place in the league, nine points ahead of fourth-placed West Ham.

It was a different story in the London Cup, however, as, after their home and away wins over Harringay in the first round, New Cross did the same to Walthamstow in the semi-final, winning the home leg 69-38 and the away leg 65-41 to give them an overall 139-74 victory. This time, the hero of the two ties was Stan Greatrex, who scored an 18-point maximum in each. Meanwhile, in the other semi-final, West Ham pulled off a surprise victory over Wembley, which was good news for New Cross as it gave them a real chance of their first major trophy in their first year at the Old Kent Road.

The first leg of the final was held at New Cross on 19 September. Once again, Johnson and Farndon led the fight for the home team with paid 17 and 15 points respectively, Farndon suffering a fall in his last race. But they received magnificent support and, in fact, the best pairing on display was the Greatrex/Key partnership, which scored 22. Key had been a little off form in the previous few matches but returned with a bang in this match, scoring 13, paid 14. The final score of 62-44 gave the Lambs an 18-point lead to defend at Custom House.

The return leg took place six days later. This was a much closer affair with home riders Bluey Wilkinson and Tommy Croombs in particular taking the fight to their opponents, but Key's return to form continued and the Lambs lost by a solitary point, 53-52, giving them a 17-point victory on aggregate, 114-97. So for the second time in their history, the Crystal Palace/New Cross team took the London Cup, a feat only achieved by one other team, Wembley.

The 1934 season had been a good year for New Cross. Following their move to the small Old Kent Road circuit after the wide-open spaces of the Crystal Palace track, the team had settled down quickly. All six of the normal team could be match-winners at times, but it was Farndon who had proved himself to be the undoubted star and was now being openly spoken of as the greatest rider in the world.

Third place in the league, behind the recognised 'super' teams of the sport, Belle Vue and Wembley, and triumph in the London Cup, gave much cause for celebration down the Old Kent Road and high hopes for the future if the team could stay together.

1934 – National League

18 April	H	West Ham	W	32-21
21 April	A	Belle Vue	L	25-26
24 April	A	Birmingham	L	25-28
25 April	H	Harringay	W	29-25
1 May	A	Plymouth	W	31-23
2 May	H	Birmingham	W	26-24
7 May	A	Wimbledon	L	24-29
9 May	H	Plymouth	W	32-22
16 May	H	Wembley	L	24-29
21 May	A	Lea Bridge	W	33-18
23 May	H	Lea Bridge	W	38-16
29 May	A	West Ham	L	26-27
6 June	H	Belle Vue	W	31-21
9 June	A	Harringay	W	33-20
13 June	H	Wimbledon	W	30-24
2 July	A	Wimbledon	W	28-25
4 July	H	Wembley	W	28-26
11 July	H	Belle Vue	L	20-34
19 July	A	Wembley	L	20-33
31 July	A	Birmingham	L	23-30
8 August	H	Walthamstow	W	36-17
14 August	A	Plymouth	W	32-21
15 August	H	Harringay	W	39-14
22 August	H	West Ham	W	29-25

5 September	H	Birmingham	W	33–21
13 September	A	Walthamstow	W	30–23
15 September	A	Harringay	W	27.5–26.5
20 September	A	Wembley	L	25–28
26 September	H	Plymouth	W	42–9
3 October	H	Wimbledon	W	38–16
6 October	A	Belle Vue	L	26–28
16 October	A	West Ham	L	21–33

P32 W21 D0 L11
For 936.5 points; Against 762.5 points
Finished 3rd (out of 9)

1934 – ACU Cup

First round

Bye

Second round

12 September	H	Wimbledon	W	62–44★

★ Match originally ended 63–43 but was subsequently amended by the ACU

Semi-final

2 October	A	West Ham	L	49–58

1934 – National Trophy

First round

Bye

Second round

26 June	A	West Ham	W	59.5–48.5
27 June	H	West Ham	W	69–36

Won 128.5–84.5 on aggregate

Semi-final

25 July	H	Wembley	L	42–62
26 July	A	Wembley	L	40-5–67.5

Lost 129.5–82.5 on aggregate

1934 – London Cup

First round

14 July	A	Harringay	W	63–44
1 August	H	Harringay	W	66–41

Won 129–85 on aggregate

Semi-final

29 August	H	Walthamstow	W	69–38
30 August	A	Walthamstow	W	65–41

Won 134–79 on aggregate

Final

19 September	H	West Ham	W	62–44
25 September	A	West Ham	L	52–53

Won 114–97 on aggregate

1934 – National League Averages*

Rider	M	R	Pts	BP	T	CMA	FM	PM
Tom Farndon	32	96	240.5	1	241.5	10.06	14	1
Ron Johnson	30	87	159	16	175	8.05	2	5
Nobby Key	31	92	156	25	181	7.87	0	6
Joe Francis	29	86	137	14	151	7.02	3	1
Stan Greatrex	32	93	147	12	159	6.84	4	1
George Newton	23	62	56	18	74	4.77	0	0
Roy Dook	11	22	15	4	19	3.45	0	0
Harry Shepherd	13	32	24	0	24	3.00	0	0

* Qualification for inclusion in all averages in the book is six matches.

1935

There were no changes in the team announced at the beginning of the 1935 season. In riding order, therefore, the team was Johnson, Francis, Greatrex, Key, Farndon, Newton, with Dook and Shepherd at reserve. Also joining the team from Plymouth as an extra reserve was Bill Stanley.

To try and give them that extra edge that would give them the league title, the mechanics, Hall and Cole, hit on the idea of rebuilding each rider's machine to suit him personally. This necessitated the complete reconstruction of many of the frames.

The season opened at the Old Kent Road track on 10 April with an individual trophy, the Jubilee Cup. With Johnson winning the cup, everything looked well set for a good season for the Lambs. However, things didn't quite turn out as expected and in their very first league match, three nights later, they were easily beaten by Harringay at their Green Lanes track. In the new 12-heat format, introduced that year for league matches, the Lambs went down 44-27, in spite of a 12-point maximum from Farndon.

New Cross's fortunes revived in their first home match against West Ham, when they won 43-29. The West Ham rider, Ken Brett, who was later to play a role in the New Cross story, suffered a very unlucky Heat 10. After a crash involving himself, his teammate, Croombs, and Francis, he was knocked out. The race was stopped and there was a delay while he recovered and the race was rerun. In the second running of the race he fell again and was knocked unconscious again.

Not surprisingly, the Lambs failed to win their next match away at Belle Vue, but, in front of a crowd of 23,000, it was said to have been one of the most exciting matches of all time with passing and repassing in every heat and not one race that could be described as a procession. The final score of 41-30 to the Aces would most probably have been a bit closer had Farndon not fallen victim to a strange refereeing decision in Heat 6. In that heat, he got off to a real flyer and had to duck under the tapes to avoid breaking them and got himself excluded. The normal practice in 1935 was to have a restart with all four back if this happened but for some reason the steward decided to exclude the New Cross star. An appeal against the exclusion was later rejected by the Control Board.

In the next home meeting, Farndon completed the set of track records. He already held the four-lap rolling-start record, the two-lap rolling-start and the one-lap flying start and in the match against Hackney Wick on 1 May, he also took the four-lap clutch-start record from Jack Parker, with a time of 60.4 seconds on his way to a maximum.

By now, New Cross had recovered from their shock defeat at the hands of Harringay at the beginning of the season and were up to second place in the league. Once again, it looked as though Belle Vue would be too strong for the rest of the league, but there were high hopes down the Old Kent Road that they could at least take the runners-up spot in the league and retain the London Cup, especially as Wembley were without Colin Watson, Harry Whitfield and George Greenwood from their 1934 team.

Shortly afterwards, New Cross were involved in a minor controversy when the Australian ACU protested about the track being selected to hold the second Test match; they felt it was unfair to their team as New Cross was so small and their riders were used to much bigger circuits.

New Cross kept up the pressure on their rivals by taking a thrilling last-heat victory at West Ham. When the riders came to the line for the twelfth and final heat, the scores were level at 33-33. With the Hammers putting out probably their best two riders, in Bluey Wilkinson and Tiger Stevenson, against Johnson and the reserve Shepherd, it looked odds-on a West Ham victory, but Johnson shot out of the gate like a rocket and although Wilkinson flew after him he could not catch the New Cross captain, who went on to win. More importantly, behind them Stevenson and Shepherd were going at it hammer and tongs with never more than a machine's length between them, as first one led and then the other, until Stevenson hit a large bump on the third lap which catapulted him up into the air, over the handlebars and deposited him on the track leaving the way clear for Shepherd to take the vital third place. Ironically, however, just one second later, Shepherd lost his chain and failed to finish. Nevertheless it was a 3-2 score to New Cross, giving them the victory.

Another win at home followed, this time 38-33 over Wimbledon. Francis had a bit of a torrid time of it in this match. In Heat 5, his throttle jammed and he shot onto the centre green, skilfully managing to avoid everybody and everything until he was able to stop. Then, in Heat 10, he led all the way until the final straight when, with about ten yards to go, he fell for no apparent reason. On the plus side, however, Farndon created another speedway landmark in the same match when he won the second heat in 59.6 seconds, the first time the one-minute mark had been beaten from a standing start on any track in the country.

To the great astonishment of the speedway world, the England selectors left Farndon out of the team to race Australia in the first Test match on 6 June. What made this decision even more bizarre was that either side of the Test match, on 5 and 7 June,

New Cross's charismatic hero,
Tom Farndon, who signed up for
Crystal Palace in 1931 and stayed
with them and New Cross until
his untimely death in 1935.

Farndon was defending his Individual Match Race title, so there was no question of
him being unfit.

As it happened, those match races themselves turned into a bit of a farce. The chosen
challenger was Hackney Wick's Australian star, Dicky Case. In the first leg at New
Cross, Case fell in both legs, giving Farndon a 2–0 victory. In the second leg, two days
later, at Hackney, the first race had to be started four times before they finally got away
only for Case to fall yet again, this time on the first bend. Farndon was now just one
race away from retaining his title, his opponent having fallen in all three races so far.
However, in the second race of the second leg, Case managed to get away first and
came out of the second bend in front with Farndon hanging on just behind. On the
first bend of the second lap, Farndon tried to cut inside Case and clipped the latter's
rear wheel, and was thrown headlong into the fence. This time it was Case who
finished alone. In the deciding race, Farndon once again fell at exactly the same spot
and so Case levelled the series at 1–1, though in fact it was more like a wrestling score
with Farndon having the advantage, three falls to two.

The deciding round was held at Wembley on 27 June. Twenty-two coach-loads of supporters, a record for away supporters at any track, travelled to the Empire Stadium to cheer their hero on. This time it was a much better contest. In the first race, Case got a tremendous start and was a length up on Farndon at the first bend. Farndon tried to sweep round the outside of Case on the first and second bends but only managed to lose more ground to the Hackney man. However, he made up ground on the back straight and got inside Case on the third bend. From then on he pulled away, winning by thirty yards and smashing the Wembley rolling-start four-lap record to smithereens. In the second race, Case again got away first, but Farndon held the inside and passed Case coming into the back straight. On the second lap, Case made a do–or–die effort to pass Farndon, but overdid it and fell, leaving Farndon to come home alone and retain his British Individual Match Race title.

While Farndon was maintaining his hold on the title, one of his teammates was winning a title of his own, as Stan Greatrex became the Dutch Champion on Whit Monday, beating fellow Lamb Nobby Key into second place. Greatrex and Key had been regular visitors to Holland in 1934 and at the beginning of 1935, so it was no surprise that they should take first and second places.

Back in the league, New Cross had a disastrous night, losing out at home to their great rivals, Wembley. Johnson was already ruled out of the match with an injured knee from a previous crash, Key was injured in a fall in the second heat, fracturing his wrist putting him out for the rest of the evening and acting captain Farndon suffered a fall and an engine failure. Surprisingly, it was Newton – who had not had a good start to the season – who put up the most spirited display for the Lambs, scoring 10 paid 11 points. The final score was New Cross 34, Wembley 38.

Farndon returned to the English Test team for the second Test at New Cross, Australia's protest having been dismissed, and showed that he should never have been left out of the first Test by scoring 14 points, the highest score on either side. The attendance at the New Cross Test turned out to be the highest Test attendance of the year, which the Control Board felt vindicated their decision not to uphold Australia's protest about the track being used.

That year's Star Championship was run along different lines than hitherto. At the suggestion of New Cross promoter Cecil Smith, in his other capacity as secretary to the Control Board, 24 top riders were chosen to compete in qualifying rounds at all the National League tracks, with the top 16 riders going through to the final, which would be held on the 20-heat, five-rides-each formula. Although Farndon was now the undoubted star of British speedway, Johnson had regained much of his old form and they formed a potent duo when both were fit. With strong backing from Francis, Greatrex and Key, New Cross was definitely a force to be reckoned with, in spite of the odd loss. Sadly, one of those losses came against Wembley yet again, this time at the Empire Stadium, but the Lambs were far from disgraced and put up a fighting performance, controversially going down 39-33 on the night, but 38-34 after a protest was upheld by the Control Board. The first controversy came in Heat 3 when Wembley's Eric

Tom Farndon in action, leading Hackney's George Wilks.

Gregory ran into Farndon and the pair of them went down. Even the home crowd were surprised that Gregory's exclusion light didn't come on. But it didn't, and he managed to remount. However, there was worse to come as he then rode a considerable distance on the grass, rejoined the track and finished a belated third and was awarded one point by the steward for doing so. The second controversy came in Heat 11. Greatrex fell on the first bend and the Wembley pair, Frank Charles and Bronco Dixon, ran into him. The race was stopped but, once again, no exclusion light came on, even though the cause of the stoppage was clearly down to Greatrex. What followed next was just pure farce. Charles, who had been badly shaken in the crash, was not fit enough to come out for the rerun for some considerable while, but the steward, Mr Alan Day, did nothing for over ten minutes. He then told the announcer to tell the crowd that, 'according to the rules, Frank Charles has one minute left to get ready'. In fact, this was quite contrary to the rule in question (Regulation No. 121), which said that: 'In the event of delay, any rider not prepared to start within two minutes after being called on by the steward through the announcer shall be excluded from the race.' The steward, who had done nothing for over ten minutes was now giving Charles only one minute instead of the required two to get to the start. In the end, Charles took another four minutes and twenty seconds to reach the start. Of course, he should have been excluded, but Mr Day let him go and he finished the race in second place. Mockford immediately slapped in a protest on two grounds, firstly that Gregory's point from Heat 3 should be removed and secondly Charles' two points in Heat 11. When the Control Board met two weeks later they dismissed the first protest but upheld the second. Charles was therefore excluded and a 4-2 to New Cross changed to a 5-1.

New Cross's next home meeting saw Tom Farndon defending his London Riders' Championship. As expected, two of the three finalists were Farndon and Johnson, who had both scored maximum points. They were joined in the final by Wally Lloyd, who had also scored the full amount. The final itself was a bit of a damp squib as Farndon shot into the lead, Lloyd fell on the second lap and Johnson, being so far behind by that stage, made no real effort to catch his teammate, thus enabling Farndon to retain the title he had won in 1934.

New Cross drew the short straw in the National Trophy first round and found themselves up against Belle Vue. Although the Aces were hot favourites to go through to the next round, the two matches turned out to be speedway classics. The first leg was at New Cross and the home team got off to a great start as Johnson and Dook took a 4-2 in Heat 1 with Johnson riding one of the races of his life to beat Eric Langton as he lost and regained the lead several times. Farndon and Newton followed this up with another 4-2 in Heat 2 , but it wasn't so much the 4-2 that sent the Old Kent Road crowd delirious as Farndon's winning time of 58.4 seconds, an incredible 1.2 seconds faster than his own track record. During the course of the race, Farndon did not vary his course by more than a few inches over the four laps. It was as near a perfect ride round the Frying Pan as you could ever hope to see. Heat 10 saw another sensational ride, this time from Johnson, who fell on the opening lap and remounted. In doing so he found himself almost a complete lap behind but he made up all of the ground on the second-placed Belle Vue rider, Bob Harrison, and even managed to pass him to take third place. Johnson's speed over the three-and-a-bit laps must have equalled, if not surpassed, Farndon's track-record speed. By Heat 13, Belle Vue had gone into a two-point lead, which they further extended over the next four heats, so that the position before the final heat was that the Aces led, 53-49, meaning that New Cross needed a 5-1 to tie the encounter. As the tapes rose, Farndon and Newton hurled themselves into the first corner followed closely by their two opponents, Bill Kitchen and Oliver Langton. From then on, the four riders were locked together for four laps with barely a machine's length between them, but the two New Cross riders just managed to hold off the other two, and Farndon came in less than a length in front of Newton, who himself was less than a length in front of Kitchen. It had been a classic encounter and the 54-54 final score was a fair result.

The away leg followed three days later on the hottest day of the year and it proved to be yet another memorable match. For most of the 1935 season and the season before, Belle Vue had seldom been extended on their own track, but this time the Lambs took the fight to their opponents. Johnson and Farndon, in particular, outrode their opponents and by the halfway point, New Cross led by seven points. Racing during the second half brought the home supporters to fever pitch as their team tried to overhaul the Lambs. By the time the final heat came round, the score was Belle Vue 52, New

Cross 49. A 5-1 to New Cross would still give them victory, not only in this leg, but also overall. The atmosphere was electric and, as the riders rode out on to the track, the noise was almost unbearable as the cheering from both sets of supporters echoed around the stadium. The New Cross pair was Farndon and Newton, while the whole of Manchester was relying on Joe Abbot and Acorn Dobson. It was Abbot who trapped first and, in spite of a determined effort, Farndon could find no way past. Newton came in third, but a 3-3 was not good enough. It had been a magnificent effort by the men from the Old Kent Road, who had given the Aces a real fright. Johnson, in particular, was in sparkling form, recording an 18-point maximum. It was only on the train home that Johnson revealed he had been riding with a displaced cartilage in his right knee and a badly swollen left foot. Johnson continued his brilliant run by tying for first place in the New Cross round of the Star Riders' championship with Jack Parker. He then followed this up with a 15-point maximum in the Harringay round.

Back in league action, New Cross did their chances of finishing runners-up no end of good as they defeated Wembley 40-31. Both Johnson and Farndon contributed their, by now, expected maximums, while Francis gave strong support with 10 points.

The next week, the Lambs scored a brilliant away win at Wimbledon, 42-29. Once again, the trio of heat leaders did their bit – Johnson knocked 1.2 seconds off the Wimbledon track record – but this time they received much better support, with Greatrex scoring seven and reserve Mike Erskine, who had been brought into the team over the previous few matches, also rode well for his two points from two rides.

The final round of the Star Riders' Championship was held at West Ham the following week, after which the Wembley qualifiers were announced. Bluey Wilkinson was top qualifier with Farndon second. Johnson, who had missed his first qualifying round through injury, nevertheless qualified in sixth place. The next night, Farndon met his next challenger for the British Individual Match Race title, Belle Vue's Max Grosskreutz, at New Cross and won both legs fairly easily.

In the return leg at Belle Vue, Grosskreutz got the better of Farndon in the first leg by something like 15 lengths. This first run showed Farndon that his opponent had a much higher gearing than himself and so he decided he had to slow up the approach to the starting line for the rolling start. This tactic led to no fewer than five false starts. On the sixth attempt, Farndon was caught by surprise as he thought the same had happened again and fully expected the red light to come on, however, it didn't and Grosskreutz shot away leaving Farndon standing. Grosskreutz was so far in front that, in spite of riding the last two laps on a flat tyre, he still managed to win.

The final and deciding leg was held at Hackney on 19 August. In the first race, Grosskreutz drew the inside berth and quickly established a commanding lead to win in a new track-record time. Farndon fought back in the second race, thus taking the decider to a third race. This time Farndon won the toss and chose the inside, but although Farndon got away first, Grosskreutz managed to get inside him round the first and second bends and shot away down the back straight with a healthy lead. But Farndon gradually pulled back the deficit and eventually swept round past Grosskreutz to come home first, thus retaining his title. Farndon had now retained his title through five challenges; no other rider had managed to successfully defend the title even once! Farndon was now at the peak of his career and certainly one of the hot favourites, if not the favourite, to win the Star Riders' Championship for the second time.

On 20 August, New Cross were away at West Ham in the first leg of their second-round London Cup tie. It was to prove a disastrous match for the Lambs, as both Francis and Shepherd were injured and found themselves out for the rest of the season. Mockford put in an official complaint to the Control Board about the state of the track and demanded compensation from West Ham for the loss of two of his riders. The following night was the second leg back at home. This was the first home meeting that Joe Francis had ever missed in eight years as a Crystal Palace or New Cross rider. In a surprise announcement, Mockford told the crowd that his place was being taken by Roger Frogley, one of Crystal Palace's original stars from 1928–1931, who had agreed to take time off from running his Herts & Essex Aerodrome at Hoddesdon to help his old club out.

With the Star Riders' final due on 29 August at Wembley, New Cross took on Harringay in a league match the evening before. Surprisingly, the Lambs lost the match 30-41, but no one who was there that night gave any thought to the result afterwards. In the second half of the match, Farndon, along with Johnson, Greatrex and West Ham's Bluey Wilkinson qualified for the final of the New Cross Scratch Race. As the tapes went up, Wilkinson, probably mindful of the following day's final, for which he too was reckoned amongst the favourites, hung back and let the three New Cross riders go. It was Johnson who took the early lead while Farndon hung on to his back wheel. It was typical of the pair that, in spite of the Star Riders' final, they still went flat out, neither wishing to be beaten, even in a scratch race. As they entered the back straight on the third lap, Johnson failed to correct a skid and crashed into the safety fence, bouncing back on to the track. With no chance of avoiding him, Farndon crashed into his teammate while broadsiding at full speed and was thrown heavily over the handlebars, landing on his head. Both Johnson and Farndon were rushed to the Miller General Hospital in Greenwich where Johnson was found to have escaped serious injury. For Farndon however, it was very different. He was found to be in a critical condition. The hospital was besieged first by hundreds and then, as the news spread, by thousands of fans. Regular bulletins on his condition were posted on the gates and bus and tram drivers stopped outside the hospital so that their passengers could read the notices.

Sadly, Farndon never regained consciousness and died two days later. By 10 p.m. the crowds had grown so large at the hospital gates that police had to be called to control them. Many of his fans collapsed with grief and had to receive medical attention themselves. One said: 'Everyone loved Tom Farndon, he was such a wonderful rider and one of the cleanest and most unspoilt stars of the tracks.'

It was the biggest tragedy to strike the sport in its seven years of existence in this country. The sport had lost probably its best rider and its finest ambassador in a meaningless race just one day before the meeting that could have cemented Farndon's place as the all-time no.1 of speedway.

At the meeting the following week, Fred Mockford told the crowd:

The passing of Tom Farndon has removed from our midst one who we can never replace, either as a rider or as a friend. As a rider his record needs no words of mine to extol – posterity will know him, not only as the finest rider of all time, but as a traditional British gentleman and sportsman. His interests were wrapped up in New Cross – not only in the track, the team and his fellow riders and management but he was the friend of the supporters as a whole… He was never too occupied to talk with you, to laugh with you and to share your personal thoughts, and many of you have enjoyed his advice and succour as we have ourselves…

Thousands lined the route on the day of his funeral. It was a tragic blow to New Cross and knocked the stuffing out of the other riders and the fans. The rest of the season was meaningless and they lost every single one of their subsequent matches, falling from second to one from bottom in the league. But no one really cared.

As a final mark of respect, the ACU agreed to abandon the British Individual Match Race competition so that Tom Farndon's name would stand in perpetuity as the unbeaten holder of the trophy.

1935 – National League

13 April	A	Harringay	L	27-44
24 April	H	West Ham	W	43-29
27 April	A	Belle Vue	L	30-41
1 May	H	Hackney Wick	W	43-24
3 May	A	Hackney Wick	W	43-29
14 May	A	West Ham	W	36-35
15 May	H	Belle Vue	L	31-40
22 May	H	Wimbledon	W	38-33
5 June	H	Harringay	W	38-33
12 June	H	Wembley	L	34-38
27 June	A	Wembley	L	33-39
29 June	A	Harringay	L	29-43
22 July	A	Hackney Wick	W	41-31
24 July	H	Wembley	W	40-31
31 July	H	Hackney Wick	L	35-37
10 August	A	Wimbledon	W	42-31
14 August	H	Wimbledon	W	43-28
17 August	A	Belle Vue	L	25-47
28 August	H	Harringay	L	30-41
31 August	A	Wimbledon	L	30-41
4 September	H	West Ham	L	35-37

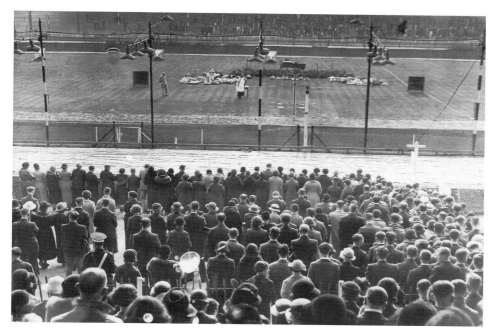

The scene at New Cross for Tom Farndon's funeral service.

5 September	A	Wembley	L	22–50
17 September	A	West Ham	L	28–43
25 September	H	Belle Vue	L	25–47

P24 W10 D0 L14
For 821 points; Against 890 points
Finished 6th (out of 7)

1935 – ACU Cup

17 April	H	Harringay	L	41–67
29 May	H	Hackney Wick	W	63–44
8 June	A	Harringay	L	45–62
21 June	A	Hackney Wick	W	62–42
26 June	H	West Ham	W	66–42
2 July	A	West Ham	L	52–53

P6 W3 D0 L3
For 329 points; Against 310 points
Finished second in group stage. Did not qualify for final.

1935 – National Trophy

First round

10 July	H	Belle Vue	D	54-54
13 July	A	Belle Vue	L	55-52

Lost 106-109 on aggregate

1935 – London Cup

First round

Bye

Semi-final

20 August	A	West Ham	L	41.5-63.5
21 August	H	West Ham	W	58-47

Lost 99.5-110.5

1935 – National League Averages

Rider	M	R	Pts	BP	T	CMA	FM	PM
Tom Farndon	19	76	182	3	185	9.74	5	1
Ron Johnson	18	72	152	6	158	8.78	4	2
Joe Francis	18	72	120	9	129	7.17	0	0
Stan Greatrex	24	94	129	9	138	5.87	1	0
Nobby Key	12	42	43	8	51	4.86	0	0
George Newton	21	75	79	7	86	4.59	0	0
Harry Shepherd	13	35	29	8	37	4.23	0	0
Roger Frogley	6	23	14	9	23	4.00	0	0
Mike Erskine	9	31	24	4	28	3.61	0	0
Roy Dook	8	20	12	3	15	3.00	0	0

1936

Mockford and Smith now faced the seemingly impossible task of finding a replacement for Farndon. All of the world's top riders were already signed up for other British teams, but over the winter news was coming through of two American brothers, Jack and Cordy Milne, who were taking the speedway world by storm out in Australia. With nothing to lose, the New Cross management signed them up for the 1936 season. The rest of the 1935 team re-signed for the club, including Norman Evans who had arrived from Wembley late the previous season, plus Ernie Evans, a former Sheffield, Belle Vue and Wimbledon rider.

As well as looking at the top end, Mockford and Smith were also keen to bring on the youngsters. Already Newton, Dook and Erskine had progressed well through the junior ranks, but now they were looking to bring on real beginners. In a statement to the Press, Cecil Smith said:

The problem of ensuring an adequate supply of first-class riders to replace weak links and the cracks when riders retire is a difficult one. The primary snag is not that there are no prospective riders, but that the existing tracks have not the facilities to give novices the experience they need. Many prospective riders naturally are not prepared to put down anything up to £100 for a machine and riding equipment unless they are assured of a real opportunity of proving and developing their worth. The tracks on their part are not generally prepared to give any opportunity unless the applicant has all the necessary equipment. In common with all the tracks, we at New Cross have been trying to find the solution for some years, and we believe we have now found it at High Beech, where our Speedway Training School is in full swing practically every day of the week and all the year round.

As Smith said, the New Cross management had started the school during the winter in the hope of unearthing talent they could use to back up their team, as and when needed. When they first published details of the school, the previous October, they were flooded with applications. On the first day of opening, within ten minutes of the start, the youngsters had written off four pairs of forks, seven tanks and one complete frame. At the time it was the only proper speedway school in existence.

Up to 20,000 spectators turned up to the opening match on 1 April, which also happened to be the first speedway fixture anywhere in the country that year. The Wimbledon pair of Geoff Pymar and Gus Kuhn won a Team Best Pairs event, beating the New Cross pairs, Newton and Norman Evans and Johnson and Francis. In the second half, one of the winter discoveries, nineteen-year-old Harry Collins, won the novices' race from Tom Farndon's brother, Syd.

Although once again the racing was excellent, things were not going quite so well behind the scenes. Firstly, the Control Board had decided not to allow both Milnes to go to New Cross; they said it would make them too strong, allocating Cordy Milne to Hackney instead. Mockford and Smith were indignant at the decision, as they held the required Ministry of Labour permits for both riders following assurances from both riders that they would only come to Britain if they could ride for New Cross.

Secondly, Nobby Key, who had spent a successful winter in Australia, cabled the management suggesting that they pay his travel costs if they wished him to return. Mockford and Smith refused even to reply, let alone accede to the request, so Key took himself off to America to try the racing out there.

Thirdly, Johnson managed to break his collarbone in a crash at West Ham on Good Friday and looked set to be out of action for several weeks.

One piece of good news came on the track itself when Newton won the April Cup against such opposition as Jack Parker, Bluey Wilkinson, Tommy Croombs, Lionel Van Praag and Wally Kilmister. It was about this time that the New Cross management announced that they were changing the team's nickname from the Lambs to the Tamers. They felt the name Lambs gave the wrong impression, as in 'lambs to the slaughter', and that the Tamers would be more appropriate so they could 'tame' the Wembley Lions and the Harringay Tigers amongst others.

Newton's form continued into the first league match of the season as he scored 11 points. However, it was not surprising that with all their problems, the match ended in a 35-36 home defeat at the hands of Wimbledon. Jack Milne did not take part in the match as he and his brother had only just arrived in England. However, they did take part in the second half and Jack delighted the crowd with promise of what was in store for the team by winning his heat of the scratch race. This was after getting out of the start last and then showing some amazing speed to overtake all three of his rivals. He then repeated the same trick in the final.

Milne's first appearance in New Cross colours came in the next match, an away meeting with Wimbledon. He scored six points from his three rides including one win.

Nobby Key rode for
Crystal Palace and New
Cross from 1931 to 1937.

But again it was another loss for New Cross as they went down 31–40. After these two losses things started to look even worse. Although Key had by now returned to England, he was still demanding money from New Cross to pay for his fare and, until it was settled, refusing to ride for them. At the same time, Francis was considering retirement and was only prepared to ride in home matches.

The first win of the season came on 29 April when the Tamers overcame Hackney Wick at home, 39-30. Newton put on another great performance to score 11 points, while Greatrex scored a maximum.

With Key's continued refusal to ride for them, Mockford and Smith took the matter to the Control Board, who reprimanded Key and informed him that, if he attempted to ride for any team other than New Cross or, in any individual meeting anywhere in the world, his licence would be 'in jeopardy'. Still in a parlous state, New Cross's next two matches were just the two they didn't need, as they were up against Belle Vue home and away. Predictably, the result was two more losses, 27-45 away and 35-37 at home.

The best news to come out of these two meetings was the continued good form of George Newton, who now seemed to have served his apprenticeship and was ready to step up from junior to heat leader. In the next match away at Harringay – which New Cross lost 32-40 – Newton broke the Green Lanes track record. Although not quite in the same class as Tom Farndon, he was another crowd pleaser in the same mould as his spectacular fence-scraping leg-trailing style brought the crowds to their feet just as their old hero had done. And now that he was scoring points as well, he was fast becoming the new darling of the Old Kent Road fans.

Milne, meanwhile, was having a steady start to his season, averaging around the seven-point mark. He felt that he needed to improve his starting and that to do that he needed a new frame, so he began experimenting with different types. Eventually, he found what he was looking for, and in the ACU Cup match against Wimbledon on 13 May, he at last came good, winning three races to help New Cross to a 51-45 win.

Johnson made his long-awaited return in the away leg. He was put in as reserve to ease his way back and scored seven points. This match saw a spectacular comeback from New Cross as, after nine heats, they were 11 points behind but from then on, they only lost one more heat, Newton and Milne winning two each, giving the Tamers a much-needed victory, albeit by one point, 48-47.

Newton's form was such that he was chosen by the Test selectors to represent England in the first Test at Wembley. In a sensational debut, Newton top-scored with 16 points, bringing England home, 65-43.

1936 saw the inauguration of the World Championship, which took the place of the Star Riders' Championship. In a genuine attempt to make it a real world championship, riders from as many countries as possible were invited to take part, although all the qualifying rounds and the final were held in Great Britain. The two foreign riders who were drawn at the New Cross qualifier were Romanians, Ionescu Cristea and Ovidiu Ionesco.

Unfortunately, it was in the West Ham round of the World Championship that Jack Milne suffered a setback that was to keep him out for a month and give him a permanent disability. During the second half he was racing against Phil Bishop when the latter fell going into the pits bend. Milne swerved to avoid him, crashing into the fence. Staggering to his feet, he noticed that his left thumb had been ripped clean off his hand. When his brother later visited him in Poplar Hospital he found Jack very depressed, saying that he was finished as a speedway rider and that it was just too big a handicap for him, as it would be impossible for him to grasp the handlebars properly. Cordy said that was nonsense and, gripping the rail at the end of the bed without using his thumb, he said: 'Look, you don't need your thumb.' Jack tried it and although his grip was weak at first, he continued to practise all the time he was in hospital. Doctors had thought it would take three months before he could use his hand again, but Jack was out of the hospital and back on the track within five weeks, acting as if nothing had happened.

Key was still refusing to ride for New Cross, although he was a regular spectator at the track. He had put in a transfer request which had been turned down both by New Cross and the Control Board. The ACU stated that they would not give him a licence until he re-signed for the Tamers. Once he had done that, they said, he could then apply for a transfer, but not before.

Johnson confirmed that he was back in form in the first round of the National Trophy as he contributed a paid maximum to New Cross's 55-51 home victory over Hackney Wick and a further 12 points plus two falls in the second leg. Taking a slender four-point lead into this tie, it always looked to be an uphill struggle for the Tamers and, in the end, Hackney Wick won 65-42, giving them a 116-97 win on aggregate.

Both Newton and Greatrex were chosen for England in the second Test match at New Cross along with Johnson for Australia. Unfortunately, Johnson crashed in his fourth ride, fracturing the same rib he had broken earlier in the season.

With no Johnson again for a while, it was fortunate that Key at last brought his long-running dispute to an end and agreed not only to sign for New Cross, but also to drop his transfer request. He lined up against West Ham, but could only manage one point. Milne, who was riding in his first match following his horrific injury, did better with seven. However, there was more trouble as West Ham defeated New Cross 49-22 and Greatrex was injured and he too was out for several matches.

With Johnson and Greatrex already missing, Francis chose this moment to announce that the time had now come for him to retire altogether, leaving the Tamers three riders down. With New Cross's next match away at Belle Vue, the whole of the speedway world was expecting a slaughter, but surprisingly, the Tamers put up probably their best showing of the season. Johnson returned for the match and contributed a useful seven points in spite of crashing heavily on the first bend in his first race. The final score was Belle Vue 36, New Cross 32, but the Tamers came very close to pulling off a remarkable draw. Going into the last heat, New Cross needed a 5-1 to tie the match and with Johnson and Milne out they had a good chance. Following his first heat fall, Johnson had scored four points in his next two races while Milne had won two of his three races and come second in his third. However, as the tapes rose, the anxious Milne reared and was thrown from his bike. Johnson won the race, showing what might have been.

On 22 July, after the match against Wimbledon, Joe Francis was presented with a gold watch in honour of his loyal years of service to the club. In his acceptance speech, Francis told the crowd that he was 'as pleased as punch' to receive the award.

At the same 22 July meeting, the Supporters' Club announced that they had some gummed paper discs for fixing to car windscreens which could be had for free from their kiosk. There was such a rush to get them that the kiosk was nearly pushed over as thousands literally fought to get their hands on the stickers.

As for the match itself that evening, it proved to be one of the most dramatic ever seen at the Old Kent Road. New Cross went behind from the start and fell even further behind as the match went on, till at one time they were eight points in arrears. Then the fightback started and, by the time the last heat came round, they were just two points

Fred Mockford explains to a group of New Cross riders how to ride the track.

behind. Johnson and Newton were out for the Tamers against the Wimbledon captain, Vic Huxley, and it was Newton who got away first, leading Huxley by a fair margin with Johnson in third place, putting New Cross into a 4-2 position but, after two laps, Newton's inexperience got the better of him and he hit the fence on the first bend of the third lap giving Huxley a clear path through, enabling Wimbledon to gain a 3-3 and the match 37-35.

New Cross's Championship round (the equivalent of the semi-final) of the World Championship was won by Newton, who took some notable scalps in so doing, including his own teammates Johnson and Milne, and Belle Vue's Eric Langton and Bob Harrison. Perhaps the biggest failure of the meeting was Wembley's Lionel Van Praag, one of the favourites for the World Championship itself, who failed to score at all in his first three rides.

New Cross's last hope for honours lay with the London Cup. Their first-round first-leg match took place on 5 August at home to West Ham and resulted in a convincing 67-41 victory. The Tamers supplied 15 out of the 18 heat winners, Newton top-scoring with 15 paid 17. Although New Cross lost the away leg six days later, it was only by 58 points to 50, so they went through to the semi-final 117-99 on aggregate.

With Johnson, Newton, Milne and Greatrex all now going well, it seemed that they could once again hold their own with the best teams. As, indeed, it proved when they comprehensively routed Wembley in their next home match, by 42 points to 30. Milne and Newton were at their brilliant best with Milne scoring a paid maximum and Newton dropping just one point to Lionel Van Praag. Heat 11 provided the crowd with some amusement as Key rolled up to the start only to find that his front tyre was flat. He frantically signalled the pits and a mechanic rushed out armed with a pump. To terrific cheers from the crowd, the mechanic pumped up the tyre at a speed bordering on a world record.

New Cross's next away match at Harringay was the cause of a very strong complaint from Mockford. He felt that the track had been watered far too much and the inner edge at one end was too wet for proper racing. There were a number of falls in the early heats and the steward halted the racing so he could make an inspection. Mockford's official letter of complaint to the Control Board said that the riders were unable to ride within 14ft of the inner edge as it was an absolute quagmire, but he also accused the Harringay manager, Tom Bradbury Pratt, of trying to deceive the New Cross riders by placing the graders and the tractor around the affected area during the opening parade so that they couldn't see how bad it was. Mockford finished his letter by saying:

> In conclusion, I will add that when I spoke to Mr Bradbury Pratt about the state of the track he stated that 'he did not know who had put all the water on'. If this is advanced as an excuse, then I maintain it is a frivolous one, as obviously a promoter or manager of a track is entirely responsible for the action of his employees.

New Cross lost the match, 33-38. The Control Board did nothing about the complaint, but later in the season both Wembley and Belle Vue also complained about the state of the Harringay track.

In spite of this wet hiccup, the New Cross boys continued their comeback with a shattering 43-27 victory over the almost hitherto invincible Belle Vue team. Once again it was the foursome of Johnson, Milne, Newton and Greatrex who stunned the Aces, with both Newton and Greatrex scoring 11 points each.

The first leg of the London Cup semi-final against Hackney Wick proved to be a real thriller, with the Tamers just coming through 54-52, but it wasn't enough to prevent Hackney progressing to the final as, in the second leg, the Wolves won by a convincing 63-43 scoreline.

There was, however, still the chance of individual glory as three New Cross riders had qualified for the first World Championship final. Newton had finished as third-highest qualifier and carried forward 12 bonus points, just one behind leading qualifier Eric Langton's 13. Jack Milne qualified with nine bonus points and Johnson with seven. Johnson had originally been first reserve but an injury to Belle Vue's Joe Abbott ruled him out and Johnson took his place. However, just three nights before the final, Johnson

George Newton, one of the most spectacular riders of all time, in action at New Cross. Newton rode for Crystal Palace and New Cross from 1931 until 1938 when a serious illness forced him to quit. He came back briefly in 1948.

fell in a challenge match at Wimbledon and damaged the shoulder he had cracked earlier in the season, putting him out of the final as well.

Up to 74,000 people, the highest-recorded attendance at any speedway match in the world, poured into Wembley stadium on 10 September to see the final. The crowd included over fifty coach-loads of fans from New Cross and when George Newton was introduced the roar of cheering was so great that anyone would have thought he was the Wembley captain. Sadly, Newton came badly unstuck very early on. He fell while last in his first ride and then reared at the start the next time out. Although he won his third race, beating Bob Harrison, Norman Parker and Ginger Lees, his dreams of the world title were already shattered. In the end he finished in ninth place with 16 points, including the 12 bonus points. Milne was one place behind him with 15 points.

There was only one thing left for New Cross in the 1936 season and that was to avoid the wooden spoon. Their next match was vital in this regard as it was against fellow strugglers West Ham. But even without Johnson, the Tamers proved too strong for their opponents and were never at any time in trouble, running out winners, 43-38. New Cross supplied the winner in every heat with Milne and Newton scoring full maximums and Greatrex a paid maximum. Even Key won a race, a rare event for him in 1936.

New Cross then proceeded to thump Harringay 44-26 and these two big wins ensured that New Cross would not finish bottom of the league. In the end, they finished three points clear of West Ham. It had been a difficult year for the Tamers but, once the team had been able to overcome its injury problems, they had settled down to become almost the force of old and there was a great air of confidence around the Old Kent Road that 1937 would be very different.

The last meeting of the season was the Tom Farndon Memorial Trophy. Although more than a year had now elapsed since Farndon's death, his memory still lived strongly in the hearts and minds of the supporters. Every Sunday, small groups would go up to Coventry to visit his grave to pay tribute to this great sportsman.

With one race to go in the meeting, Newton and Huxley had 13 points from their five rides. Only Milne, with four wins from four rides, could stop one of them from carrying off the trophy. He found himself up against Greatrex, West Ham's Eric Chitty and his brother Cordy. Up went the tapes and up went a collective cry of anguish from the crowd as Jack spluttered to a halt after a couple of yards as his chain came off. Fortunately for him, the steward was not satisfied with the start and switched on the red lights. Milne now had another chance and after some hurried work in the pits replacing his chain, he was ready to go. But, this time, after cruising up to the tapes, his machine cut out and he couldn't get it to start again. There was much running to and fro from the pits, as the two-minute warning was running out second by second. A mechanic brought out another machine and with just a few seconds to spare, Milne jumped on this one. Meanwhile, one of the other mechanics, Tommy Hall, had finally got Milne's own machine to start, so he swapped back again. This time there was no problem and Jack had an easy win to score maximum points and take the trophy. It was presented to him by Mrs Tom Farndon.

It was a fitting end to the season that a New Cross rider and especially Jack Milne, who had been brought into replace Farndon, should take New Cross's most precious trophy. Just for once, the hard-bitten business man Fred Mockford, normally to be seen striding about the centre green in his fur coat barking out orders and whipping up the crowd, was so moved that he stood motionless as the cup was presented, almost in tears.

1936 – National League

22 April	H	Wimbledon	L	35-36
25 April	A	Wimbledon	L	31-40
29 April	H	Hackney Wick	W	39-30
2 May	A	Belle Vue	L	27-45
6 May	H	Belle Vue	L	35-37
9 May	A	Harringay	L	32-40
27 May	H	West Ham	W	43-29
23 June	A	West Ham	L	22-49
24 June	H	Harringay	L	34-38
27 June	A	Belle Vue	L	32-36
8 July	H	Wembley	L	28-43
10 July	A	Hackney Wick	W	44-26
21 July	A	West Ham	L	28-44
22 July	H	Wimbledon	L	35-37
12 August	H	Hackney Wick	W	43-29
19 August	H	Wembley	W	42-30
22 August	A	Harringay	L	33-38
26 August	H	Belle Vue	W	43-27
27 August	A	Wembley	L	25-47
11 September	A	Hackney Wick	W	40-32
16 September	H	West Ham	W	43-28
17 September	A	Wembley	L	35-36
23 September	H	Harringay	W	44-26
5 October	A	Wimbledon	L	31-40

P24 W9 D0 L15

For 844 points; Against 863 points

Finished 6th (out of 7)

1936 – ACU Cup

13 May	H	Wimbledon	W	51-45
16 May	A	Wimbledon	W	48-47
3 June	H	Wembley	L	37-59
4 June	A	Wembley	L	42-54

P4 W2 D0 L2

For 178 points; Against 205

Finished second in group stage. Did not qualify for final.

1936 – National Trophy

First round

10 June	H	Hackney Wick	W	55–51
12 June	A	Hackney Wick	L	42–65

Lost 97–116 on aggregate

1936 – London Cup

First round

5 August	H	West Ham	W	67–41
11 August	A	West Ham	L	50–58

Won 117–99 on aggregate

Semi-final

2 September	H	Hackney Wick	W	54–52
4 September	A	Hackney Wick	L	43–63

Lost 97–115 on aggregate

1936 – National League Averages

Rider	M	R	Pts	BP	T	CMA	FM	PM
Jack Milne	22	88	181	10	191	8.68	1	1
George Newton	24	96	197	8	205	8.54	2	1
Stan Greatrex	21	83	167	4	171	8.24	1	2
Ron Johnson	11	44	77	8	85	7.73	0	0
Joe Francis	6	24	33	3	36	6.00	0	0
Norman Evans	24	95	99	17	116	4.88	0	0
Nobby Key	17	65	47	11	58	3.57	0	0
Harry Shepherd	13	38	24	5	29	3.05	0	0
Roy Dook	8	19	8	4	12	2.53	0	0

1937

So determined were the New Cross management to put up a better show in 1937 that they opened the track in February for the riders to get in plenty of practice before the season started. Although it was all unofficial, Newton was putting in some astonishing laps on a new frame, which he had built especially for him over the winter. In one practice he covered the four laps in 58 seconds, two-fifths of a second inside Farndon's official track record. Greatrex and Ernie Evans had also had new frames built and were trying them out in practice.

Two new young Canadian riders, Johnnie Millet and Harold Bain, were having their first taste of English tracks at New Cross before moving on to Bristol. New Cross and Bristol, under promoter Ronnie Greene, had a close relationship, with Bristol being an unofficial New Cross second team. Already, in the previous year, Shepherd, Dook and Erskine had turned out regularly for the Bulldogs.

Once again New Cross was given the honour of holding the first speedway meeting of the season on 31 March. However, the spring of 1937 saw some very bad weather and the meeting was snowed off.

From the previous year's team, New Cross retained Stan Greatrex, who was elected captain by the riders themselves; George Newton, elected vice-captain; Jack Milne, Norman Evans, Ernie Evans, Nobby Key, Jack Dalton, Henry Collins and Will Lowther. Clem Mitchell was also shown on the retained list but there was still some dispute with West Ham over who he would ride for, with the Control Board being asked to make a final decision. In a surprise move, Joe Francis had decided to come out of retirement and he too was on the list. The main figure missing was former captain Ron Johnson, as there was still some uncertainty about whether he would return from Australia. Also missing was Harry Shepherd, another rider, like Johnson and Francis, who had been with the club since 1928.

As well as naming the team for the year, Mockford and Smith also announced that, henceforth, the team were to be known as the Rangers, 'Call 'em Lambs and they behave like those timid beasts and finish near the foot of the league table,' said Mockford. He added that complaints had been made that the Tamers made them sound 'tame', so they had changed the name to the Rangers, the name they were to keep until the final closure in 1963. In an effort to improve presentation and in true showmanship style, Mockford decreed that all the team's bikes had to be copperplated.

The New Cross season eventually got underway with the traditional opening best-pairs meeting and, in front of the biggest crowd they had yet had for the first night, local riders Newton and Ernie Evans won by the skin of their teeth, just managing to hold off Harringay's Jack Parker and Frank Goulden.

As New Cross were preparing for their first official fixture of the season, news came through that Ron Johnson was returning after all but his future was not entirely clear as Wimbledon had put in a bid for his services. The matter was left in the hands of the Control Board.

After all the hopes for the season, the first match lived up to all expectations as the Rangers scored a very convincing 49.5-34.5 victory over Harringay. A new 14-heat formula had been introduced for the season, with eight riders per team. The New Cross team for this opening match was Greatrex, Newton, Milne, Key, Francis, Norman Evans, Ernie Evans and Dalton. Newton scored a maximum, while Milne and Greatrex both reached double figures.

Although they lost their next match away at West Ham, they followed this up with a string of five consecutive victories, including wins over Belle Vue and Wembley at home and two away. In the 51-33 win over Belle Vue, the three stars once again came good, this time Milne scored the maximum. Newton followed up with a maximum away at Hackney Wick. From then on, it was all Milne as he put together a string of seven consecutive maximums, including three away from home. There was no doubt that Milne was now becoming the rider of the season, unbeatable at home and virtually so away. But unlike Newton, or Farndon before him, Milne was not an exciting rider to watch, tending to ride with his head, waiting for an opening or the slightest mistake from his opponent, should that rider be in front, rather than go in for a breathless dash round the boards. In fact, it was said that Milne showed all the dash of a clockwork mouse!

A strange dispute blew up early in 1937. Until the end of 1936, New Cross had been noted throughout speedway as the team which sent most coaches to away matches. Suddenly, early in 1937, they were informed by the Traffic Commissioner that both they and the coach company who supplied their coaches, Thomas Tilling, had been breaking regulations. Tilling's crime was that they had been running the coaches too cheaply, while New Cross's crime apparently was that they had advertised the coach trips to away fixtures in the programme and over the public address. The London Passenger Transport Board (LPTB), the forerunner of London Transport and Transport for London, complained that anyone living near New Cross could get normal service

Jack Milne in action. Milne rode for New Cross from 1936 to 1939.

buses to travel to away matches and that if the Supporters' Club was to run its own coaches it had to charge the same fares, which were currently about 2s less than the LPTB buses. The Traffic Commissioner upheld this complaint.

With the form of Milne and the continued support of Newton and Greatrex, both themselves contributing maximums along the way, New Cross moved to the top of the table. Although Milne scored yet another maximum, the Rangers' run of victories came to an end with a 35-49 defeat at Harringay. But the good news for New Cross was that Johnson had returned and it had been agreed he would ride for New Cross. His return now gave New Cross promise of an even stronger team and one that might still win the league championship. Midway through the season they were in second place, four points behind West Ham.

The National Trophy was next on the agenda as the Rangers took on Harringay in the first round and slaughtered them over the two legs. Away they pulled off a magnificent 65-41 victory, while at home they just simply overwhelmed the Tigers, 76-31, and yet, for the first time in eight official matches – 35 races altogether – Milne lost a race. The man who beat him was Harringay's Clem Mitchell who, ironically, was actually a New Cross rider on loan to the Tigers. It happened in Heat 17 of the match, when Mitchell shot away from the start and led all the way. Until that point, Mitchell had scored just five points from five rides. This time it was Newton who scored a full maximum and Greatrex a paid maximum. New Cross progressed to the second round 141-72 on aggregate.

Shortly after his victory over Milne, Clem Mitchell took his place in the New Cross team, but the whole saga was a very strange one. He had originally signed up for New Cross on 8 April and his contract was eventually endorsed by the Control Board but they stipulated that he had to be loaned to Harringay until such time as either Bill Pitcher or Norman Parker returned from injury. Eventually, the news that he was to return to New Cross to ride was broken by a national newspaper and came as a surprise to both New Cross and Mitchell himself. On enquiring of the Control Board, Mockford and Smith learnt that Harringay had agreed to release him, but the Board itself had not yet validated this. It did agree that, until a final decision was made, Mitchell could be loaned back to New Cross. So, for a while, Mitchell was a New Cross rider on loan to Harringay on loan to New Cross! With the arrival of Mitchell back at his home club, Mockford agreed to let Nobby Key go to Wimbledon, thus ending a somewhat tempestuous relationship that had lasted since 1931.

Since New Cross had opened at the beginning of 1934, only one meeting had been cancelled. Nevertheless, the management decided not to take any chances and invested in a motor-driven pump, capable of removing 15,000 gallons of water per hour. The management hoped that this would prevent any further cancellations as the pump could remove water as fast as it could collect.

The Rangers did themselves the world of good with their next win, over league leaders West Ham. Milne returned to his maximum ways, but no one in the team scored less than six for a real all-round team effort to win 56-28, putting them equal with West

Ham at the top of the table. Unfortunately for the hopes of the team, the Rangers went down 29-54 to Belle Vue three days later. However, the whole meeting was the cause of a protest by Mockford, as Belle Vue were trying out a new starting technique, laying down a patch of asphalt on the line, so that it would be absolutely level and not enable the riders to dig ruts. The New Cross riders, especially Johnson, did not like it and Mockford put in an official protest.

After a big 55-28 victory over Wimbledon, the Rangers lost a close encounter with Hackney Wick at Waterden Road, by just three points. During this match it was reported in the national Press that, following the yellow exclusion light coming on in Heat 10, Greatrex took off his helmet so he could see what colour he was wearing, saw it was white, put it back on and chased after the Hackney pairing of Fred Hodgson and Dicky Case.

The strength of the New Cross team was confirmed when the qualifiers for the championship round of the World Championship was announced as every one of the New Cross riders had got through the first round. Only the Belle Vue team was able to emulate this feat. Jack Milne confirmed his current no.1 ranking by winning the London Riders' Championship.

While New Cross and West Ham were fighting it out at the top of the table, Wembley were creeping up behind them. Wembley traditionally started the season late as they had to wait until after the FA Cup final and the Rugby League Challenge Cup final had been held in the stadium. By the time they met New Cross on 8 July at the Empire Stadium, they had scored seven consecutive victories, including two away, so the match was a vital one which, sadly for the Rangers, they lost 36-47. Only Milne put up a real fight, scoring his usual maximum, including a first-heat victory over the world champion, Wembley's own Lionel Van Praag. The rest of the team had a poor evening and Milne's only real support came from reserve Ernie Evans, who scored six points from three rides including a magnificent Heat 8 win over Ginger Lees and Tommy Price.

The following week, New Cross got their revenge by knocking Wembley out of the National Trophy at the semi-final stage, winning both legs: 59-48 at home and 58-50 away. Both legs saw the Rangers at their best with solid scoring from the whole team.

The following night, however, their hopes of the league title took a blow as they lost at unfancied Harringay, 41-52. The whole complicated issue of Clem Mitchell came up again as Bradbury Pratt, the Harringay manager, objected to him riding for New Cross as he had already ridden for Harringay in the league. The steward ruled that as he was now officially on loan to New Cross, there was no objection to him riding for them.

It was rumoured about this time that Johnson would follow Nobby Key to Wimbledon. He was not having a good season. He started late and had never really seemed to catch up with the rest and even dropped down to reserve for a while. After trying out several new frames, including one built especially for him by teammate Ernie Evans, which was based on an old 1931 Wallis, he felt there was a more fundamental problem and decided to change over to the foot-forward style. As he got used to this new style, his old form began to return and he announced that he had no intention of moving to Wimbledon and wished to remain part of the New Cross set-up. For his part, Mockford welcomed this decision and expressed the hope that, with his return to form, Johnson's confidence would also return and he would once again be the rider that took the British Individual Match Race title in 1933.

On 11 August, New Cross embarked on their quest for a third London Cup with a good home victory over Wimbledon, 65-43, in the first round first leg. The Rangers were without Newton for the tie as he had been taken into hospital with food poisoning. However, the rest of the team rose to the challenge, with that man Milne scoring yet another maximum. His partnership with Mitchell was almost perfection itself, as Milne would let Mitchell gate first and then team ride him home with Mitchell easing up on the last straight to allow Milne to take the three points. They took three 5-1s in this way. Even better in many ways was the form shown by the two 'old timers' in the team. Johnson and Francis rode together as a pair and scored 23 points between them, 10 to Johnson and 13 to Francis, including three 5-1s.

The second leg was not held until 6 September but, in the meantime, the final of the National Trophy took place. The first leg at Hyde Road, Manchester, on 21 August all but settled the outcome as, in front of a record 40,000 crowd, Belle Vue took an enormous 28-point lead, winning 65-37.

Although it seemed to be over, someone forgot to tell the New Cross boys and they put up a tremendous fight in the second leg back at the old Kent Road. By the interval following the ninth heat, the Rangers had clawed back 15 points and there was a real possibility that they might just do it. But, whatever was said in Belle Vue's half-time team talk must have worked, as Belle Vue came out with a much more determined attitude in the second half. The match was won by them in the three heats, 12-14, as they took two 5-1s and one 4-2, thus ending any lingering hope New Cross might have had of snatching victory. In the end, New Cross still scored a good victory over the National Trophy winners for the previous four years, by winning the leg 62-45, but it was not enough and they lost 99-110 on aggregate.

Before the London Cup first-round second-leg match there was the little matter of the World Championship final on 2 September at Wembley. To nobody's surprise, Jack Milne had qualified as top scorer in the Championship round with 83 points, giving him 13 bonus points to carry forward. Next was Belle Vue's Eric Langton, five points behind on 78, with 12 bonus points. The only other New Cross rider to qualify was George Newton who qualified in eighth place with 67 points, equating to 11 bonus points. After the year he had had, with maximum after maximum, home and away, Milne was the red-hot favourite to take the title and, in front of a crowd of 85,000, so it came to pass. He won all his five rides comfortably, completely dominating the event and proving beyond doubt that he was the best rider in the world. Newton finished in joint-eighth place; having won his first ride – he beat the eventual third-placed rider, Cordy Milne, Bill Kitchen and 1935 Star Riders' Champion, Frank Charles – he fell in his next three rides, putting him completely out of the running.

Jack Milne with the 1937 World Championship trophy.

When the second leg of the London Cup first-round tie did eventually take place, it was a non-contest. Already 22 points up from the first leg, New Cross just pulled further and further in front with the whole team taking points as and when they pleased, giving the Rangers a 65–42 win and a 130–85 victory on aggregate.

After all the cup and world championship distractions, New Cross returned to league business with a hard-fought match against close rivals Wembley. After five heats, Wembley were four points up but a 5–1 from Newton and Norman Evans brought the scores back level. By Heat 7 it was New Cross who were four points up. At the end of Heat 12 the scores were New Cross 37, Wembley 34. In Heat 13, Francis fell on the last bend while in second place, handing Wembley a 5-1 and a one-point lead going into the last race. This heat was therefore vital for New Cross remaining with a chance of taking the league title. Lined up for the Rangers were Mitchell and Norman Evans, while Wembley put out Wally Kilmister and Tommy Price. As the tapes went up, Mitchell and Evans got away first, with Kilmister pushing hard on the first bend, but fortunately for the New Cross pair, he tried too hard and fell on the second. Mitchell and Evans rode as a pair, keeping out Price for three laps, but on the fourth lap he managed to push Mitchell out wide, finishing just behind Evans. It was a close call, but the resulting 4-2 gave the Rangers a one-point victory in the match to keep their league championship hopes alive.

The following week, however, it all came crashing down as New Cross were crushed by league leaders West Ham on their Custom House track. It started badly for the Rangers as, in the very first heat, Milne suffered mechanical problems and, for the first time that season, trailed in in last place. His second ride was one of the most amazing races ever seen at Custom House, or anywhere else for that matter. For four laps, Milne and his opponent Bluey Wilkinson raced shoulder to shoulder, never more than half a machine's length between the two. They arrived at the last bend dead level, both rocketed round it at terrific speed, Milne entering the straight a shade ahead, but Wilkinson, on the inside, just eased past on the straight as the enormous crowd rose to their feet cheering themselves hoarse to witness Wilkinson win by no more than the width of a tyre in a new track-record time. Milne won his last two races but to no avail as, apart from him, only Newton was able to resist the Hammers' onslaught, scoring nine points, including one spectacular win when, throwing caution to the wind, he went from third to last by taking the outside line, almost scraping the fence to overtake Tiger Stevenson and Tommy Croombs in one move. The final score, however, was West Ham 55 New Cross 28.

Out of the National Trophy and with no realistic chance of the League title, New Cross's one hope now was the London Cup. The first leg of the semi-final took place on 22 September against Wembley. Once again it was a case of the whole team contributing to the very fine 62-46 win. With a lead of 16 points, there were high hopes that they could keep Wembley's score down sufficiently in the second leg to reach the final.

As it happened, not only did they keep Wembley's score down at the Empire Stadium, but they even managed to pull off a stunning away victory by 56 points to 50. It was as early as the third heat that the Rangers, thanks to a 4-2 from Johnson and Newton, managed to forge ahead. It was yet another solid team performance led by Milne but backed up by the rest of the team.

The first leg of the final was just five days later at Custom House. It was not going to be an easy task for the Rangers, as they were up against the newly crowned league champions West Ham, undefeated on their own track all season. A crowd of 47,392 paid to see the match, which ended in a surprise victory for the visitors, 55-52. Part of the reason for this was the way the track had been prepared. The inside line was almost devoid of cinders and was as flat and smooth as an iron. Strangely, it was the New Cross riders, who adapted to the riding conditions first and better, but it was an unusual sight to see the normally white-line-hugging Milne take to the outside for his races. For Newton and Johnson, of course, it made very little difference as this was their preferred method of racing anyway. Once again, the races between Milne and Wilkinson proved to be the highlights of the match, both getting the better of the other once in finishes that separated them by mere inches. However, with a track perfectly suited to his style, Newton turned out to be the man of the match, scoring 17 points.

With a three-point lead to take back to the Old Kent Road, New Cross had every reason to be optimistic about the final result, but they were not over-confident as West Ham were league champions for a reason. However, they needn't have worried, as Milne, Johnson, Newton and Greatrex all finished with double figures to pull off a handsome 62-45 victory, thus taking the London Cup for the third time in their history in front of the largest crowd of the season.

In all, it had been a good year for the Rangers. Winners of the London Cup, finalists in the National Trophy and third place in the league, equal on points to runners-up Wembley. In Jack Milne, the world champion, they undoubtedly had the rider of the year and a worthy successor to Tom Farndon.

As well as becoming world champion, Milne finished top of the National League averages with an incredible 11.09 cma, having scored 14 full and two paid maximums in 22 matches. At home his average was a stunning 11.82, with eight full and two paid maximums from 11 matches. He had scored 130 paid points out of a possible total of 132. no one had ever achieved this sort of scoring before in the history of the sport.

Just one footnote to the year: in spite of Jack Milne's incredible record at home, the four-lap clutch-start track record at the end of the year still stood in the name of Tom Farndon. Perhaps that was just another tribute to that remarkable man.

1937 – National League

14 April	H	Harringay	W	49.5-34.5
20 April	A	West Ham	L	30-53
21 April	H	Belle Vue	W	51-33
23 April	A	Hackney Wick	W	42-40
28 April	H	Wimbledon	W	48-35
3 May	A	Wimbledon	W	42-40
5 May	H	Wembley	W	49-35
8 May	A	Harringay	L	35-49
13 May	A	Wembley	L	31-52
26 May	H	Hackney Wick	W	44-39
16 June	H	West Ham	W	56-28
19 June	A	Belle Vue	L	29-54
23 June	H	Wimbledon	W	55-28

2 July	A	Hackney Wick	L	40-43
8 July	A	Wembley	L	36-47
28 August	A	Harringay	W	54-30
1 September	H	Wembley	W	42-41
7 September	A	West Ham	L	28-55
8 September	H	Belle Vue	W	46-37
15 September	H	Hackney Wick	W	58-26
4 October	A	Wimbledon	W	52-31
6 October	H	Harringay	W	47-37
13 October	H	West Ham	W	47-37
16 October	A	Belle Vue	L	31-53

P24 W16 D0 L8
For 1,054 points; Against 943 points
Finished 3rd (out of 7)

1937 – ACU Cup Pool Two

5 July	A	Wimbledon	W	60-34
17 July	A	Harringay	L	41-52
28 July	H	Wimbledon	W	60-34
4 August	H	Wembley	L	47-48
5 August	A	Wembley	L	41.5-54.5
18 August	H	Harringay	W	62-34

Finished 2nd in group stage
Did not qualify for final

1937 – National Trophy

First Round

5 June	A	Harringay	W	65-41
9 June	H	Harringay	W	76-31

Won 141-72 on aggregate

Semi-final

14 July	H	Wembley	W	59-48
15 July	A	Wembley	W	58-50

Won 117-98 on aggregate

Final

| 21 August | A | Belle Vue | L | 37-65 |
| 25 August | H | Belle Vue | W | 62-45 |

Lost 99-110 on aggregate

1937 – London Cup

First round

| 11 August | H | Wimbledon | W | 65-43 |
| 6 September | A | Wimbledon | W | 65-42 |

Won 130-85 on aggregate

Semi-final

| 22 September | H | Wembley | W | 62-46 |
| 23 September | A | Wembley | W | 56-50 |

Won 118-96 on aggregate

Final

| 28 September | A | West Ham | W | 55-52 |
| 29 September | H | West Ham | W | 62-45 |

Won 117-97 on aggregate

1937 – National League Averages

Rider	M	R	Pts	BP	T	CMA	FM	PM
Jack Milne	22	88	242	2	244	11.09	14	2
George Newton	22	88	190	6	196	8.91	1	0
Stan Greatrex	21	80	164	5	169	8.45	2	1
Clem Mitchell	12	42	52	13	65	6.19	0	0
Norman Evans	24	88	109	20	129	5.86	0	1
Ron Johnson	15	59	76	10	86	5.83	0	1
Joe Francis	21	82	103	16	119	5.80	1	0
Ernie Evans	24	62	54.5	10	64.5	4.16	0	0
Nobby Key	12	39	28	4	32	3.28	0	0
Jack Dalton	8	17	8	2	10	2.35	0	0

1938

Mockford and Smith once again opened the New Cross track early for practice and were very impressed with the pre-season form of Newton, who was timed at 57 seconds for four laps in one race. Milne was trying out a new front-wheel tyre with an over-all tread which he believed gave far greater wheel grip than ordinary tyres. New signing Goldy Restall, from Canada, was also showing good form at the pre-season practices.

Mockford decided it was time to introduce a keep-fit regime and employed the Clapton Orient football team trainer, Bill Wright, to oversee this. Mockford installed the latest radiant-heat equipment, together with rowing machines, medicine balls and the like. He said that the riders were very keen to try it out.

As the season started, the New Cross retained riders were announced as Ron Johnson, Joe Francis, George Newton, Ernie Evans, Stan Greatrex, Clem Mitchell, Jack Milne, Mick Murphy, Goldy Restall and Harry Bowler. Norman Evans had left to join Wimbledon. The Supporters' Club announced that they had 13,000 members.

The Rangers got off to a flying start in their league campaign, caning Belle Vue 55-28. Milne, Newton and Greatrex all showed that they were on top form, Milne and Newton scoring maximums and Greatrex 11. Behind them came strong support from Mitchell, who scored a three-ride paid maximum, Johnson, six points and Restall, five. Also included in the New Cross line-up for the first time at reserve was a young diminutive Australian, Bill Longley, who at 5ft 1in was probably the shortest rider in speedway at that time. He scored two points in his first ride, coming in behind his partner, Jack Milne, and fell in his second. In the second half, he reached the scratch-race final and caused a sensation by leading Milne, Newton and Johnson for one-and-a-half laps before Milne managed to get past him. Try as they might,

Newton and Johnson could not find a way through. It was a very encouraging debut match for the twenty-three year old and added to the general confidence around the Old Kent Road that this was going to be their year.

Another big victory followed as the Rangers thumped Harringay, 56-28. For the second successive meeting, Milne and Newton went through the card unbeaten. Ernie Evans returned to the track in the second half, having spent the first couple of weeks of the season in hospital with appendicitis.

With their confidence sky high, New Cross travelled north to meet Belle Vue and took part in yet another exciting match on the Manchester track. The first six heats were all 3-3, but in Heat 7 and Heat 8, Belle Vue scored two 4-2 results. The next three heats were 3-3 again, but New Cross regained three points in Heat 12 as Restall finished alone for a 3-0. Milne and Kitchen had collided at the start, while Oliver Langton's chain snapped later in the race. The thirteenth heat was another 3-3, leaving New Cross one point behind with one heat to go. This final race was a real thriller, bringing the 25,000 crowd to their feet. Mitchell gated first and never looked like being headed, Harrison took second place, but it was the battle for the vital third spot that had everyone cheering like mad as Oliver Langton and Longley fought it out neck and neck for four laps, with never more that a machine's length between them. In the end it was Langton who just managed to flash across the finishing line for that crucial one point, giving Belle Vue victory by 41-40.

Although they had lost the match, New Cross were now being spoken of as firm favourites for the league title, with two big wins at home and one loss away by a single point to Belle Vue. The next home match confirmed their status as they defeated the team that everyone had to beat, Wembley. For the third successive home match, Milne scored a maximum to give the Rangers a well-deserved 45-39 victory. Longley also had another good meeting, scoring a reserve's maximum of paid six from his two rides.

New Cross narrowly lost their next away match to league champions West Ham by just two points, 39-41, but this was followed by a string of five victories, including two away, putting them firmly in the driving seat for the 1938 league championship.

In the first match of this run, Milne had the unusual experience of not winning a race. Twice he team rode his partner Mitchell home, but twice he was beaten by West Ham's Bluey Wilkinson in the Rangers' 53-30 victory. He dropped another point in the next match, away at Bristol to Bill Clibbett, but then reeled off three more maximums in the final three matches of the run, the last of which saw a fine 46-37 away victory over Wembley, with Newton also contributing maximum points.

By the end of this run, on 2 June, New Cross were firmly ensconced at the top of the league. The reason for these victories was that New Cross now had five riders of heat-leader class, with two, Milne and Newton, amongst the top ten in the league. The other factor in New Cross's exceptional performances was that the side was a very settled one. The same seven riders had turned out in every match of the season so far, the other two being Restall and Longley. The eighth spot had alternated between Bowler and Evans.

The match that brought an end to the winning run took place at Wimbledon on 13 June. For the first time this season there was a change in the top seven as Restall was replaced by Francis. But it wasn't this that caused New Cross to lose, it was the fact that Milne only scored two points. In his first race he came home second to his teammate, Mitchell, to give the Rangers the perfect 5-1 start. In his second race he was excluded for taking Wally Lloyd into the fence and in his third race he touched Geoff Pymar's back wheel, causing him to crash into the fence head-on. Although he was up on his feet almost immediately, he was unable to take part in the rest of the meeting. Mitchell, Newton, Johnson, Greatrex and Longley tried their best but the loss of so much scoring power was too big a handicap for New Cross and they went down 39-44.

With the Rangers still top, there was a short break from league action as the National Trophy got underway. New Cross's first-round tie was against Wimbledon, with the first leg at home on 7 July. Newton was missing following a fall in a second-half event at Wimbledon the previous week and Greatrex crashed heavily in his first race putting him out for the rest of the evening. Milne tried his best to stave off defeat but even his 17 points were not enough for New Cross to avoid suffering their first home defeat of the campaign as they went down 50-57. The second leg back at Wimbledon was almost a repeat of the first. Newton was out and Greatrex, still suffering from his fall five days previously, was little more than a passenger, so, once again, it was left to Milne to carry the fight with 16 points. But it was a hopeless cause and the Rangers went down and out of the National Trophy.

Although they were out of the National Trophy, the timing of the first round was a blessing in disguise as it meant that Newton only missed one league encounter and was back in time for the home match against Harringay on 13 July. With Newton now back, it was the end of a team place for Restall. After a promising start, he had not lived up to expectations and his place was taken on a permanent basis by Francis. Newton started his comeback well with two wins but then tired quickly and, after coming third in his third race, he retired from the match. Meanwhile, Milne was scoring his usual 12 points and Longley was contributing his first double-figure score with a paid maximum, winning two races and coming second behind his partner, Greatrex, twice. The Rangers were back on track for the league title with an easy 54-29 win.

A 24-59 defeat at the hands of Harringay on 30 July was to be the last loss suffered by the Rangers until 9 September. The run of five matches without defeat included two away at highly fancied Wembley and league champions West Ham, as well as home wins over the same two clubs and Bristol. Milne was, of course, the driving force in all the victories, scoring two full maximums, two paid maximums and a paid 11. But, once again, it was the strength in depth that did for New Cross's opponents with Longley scoring his first full maximum in the away match at Wembley and the same eight riders featuring in all five matches.

This run proved decisive in the league as, even with four matches still to race, New Cross were crowned champions after the victory over Bristol on 7 September. This was just as well really, because the Rangers then proceeded to lose all four remaining matches, although this could be explained partly by injuries to Greatrex and Mitchell,

Stan Greatrex, a leading rider with New Cross from 1934 to 1939 ran a motorcycle business which he often advertised in the New Cross programme.

and partly by the fact that, inevitably, some of the zest had gone out of the New Cross side after they had been confirmed as champions.

Towards the end of the season, New Cross were called on to defend the London Cup they had won in 1937. After a bye in the first round, the Rangers eased past West Ham in the semi-final, 114-102 on aggregate, and found themselves up against Wimbledon in the final.

The first leg, at New Cross, saw an end to the Rangers' losing streak as they narrowly won 55-52. New Cross increased their lead in the first heat of the return leg, as Milne and Newton took a 4-2 from Wilbur Lamoreaux and Eric Collins. Johnson won the second heat to make it 7-5 on the night and 62-57 on aggregate, but from then on the Dons slowly but surely fought back and built up a small lead until, by the last heat, they were one point up on aggregate. The last race saw Milne and Newton out for the Rangers and Lamoreaux and Benny Kaufman for Wimbledon. From the start the two Dons took the lead and for four laps the four riders fought it out with never more than two lengths covering the two Wimbledon riders and Milne. It was a sensational race, but Milne just could not find his way past and with Newton trailing badly in last place, the race finished in a 5-1 for the Dons and victory for them on the night by 57 points to 49, an overall victory of 109-104. New Cross had lost their London Cup, but had been more than compensated by the fact that they were now National League Champions for the first time in their history.

Once again, Milne had had a tremendous year, topping the averages for the second year running with a cma of 10.96. However, his World Championship reign had come to an end. This year he had qualified for the final with seven bonus points, one behind arch-rival Bluey Wilkinson's eight. The pair met in Heat 19 of the final, by which time Wilkinson had 12 points from his four rides, while Milne had 11, having been defeated by fellow American Wilbur Lamoreaux in Heat 10. Because Milne had one less bonus point than Wilkinson, it wasn't enough for him to win the race, he needed Wilkinson to come in third for a tie or fourth for outright victory.

As luck would have it, Jack Milne's brother Cordy was in the same race and Jack hoped that his brother would be able to play his part. And, sure enough, as the tapes rose, it was the two Milne brothers who got away first, but Wilkinson managed to battle his way past Cordy and, knowing that second place was good enough, let Jack go to concentrate on keeping his brother out. Time and again, Cordy tried to get past the West Ham rider but every time he was thwarted. Both Jack Milne and Wilkinson finished the evening on 14 points but that one extra bonus point made all the difference and Milne had to be content with the runner-up spot.

Newton also qualified for the final, scoring just two points on the night, to finish in joint fourteenth place. In fact, although Newton was also New Cross's second-placed rider in the averages with a cma of 8.35, it was noticeable that, towards the end of the season, he seemed to be tiring and was not quite the same rider who had started the year so positively. In fact, Newton's tiredness was due to the beginnings of a serious illness. As he did every year, he went to the South of France for a holiday as soon as racing finished but was so ill that he had had to return. On his arrival back in England he was taken to hospital where X-rays and blood tests were taken. He was ordered to take a complete rest for six months and fans were told not to bother him either by visiting him in person or even by writing to him. Although it was never stated at the time, the fact was that Newton had contracted tuberculosis and a return to racing looked extremely unlikely, though the official line was that he would be fit to resume in 1939.

1938 – National League Division One

20 April	H	Belle Vue	W	55–28
27 April	H	Harringay	W	56–28
30 April	A	Belle Vue	L	40–41
4 May	H	Wembley	W	45–39
10 May	A	West Ham	L	39–41
11 May	H	West Ham	W	53–30
20 May	A	Bristol	W	46–38
25 May	H	Bristol	W	51–33
1 June	H	Wimbledon	W	51–33
2 June	A	Wembley	W	46–37

13 June	A	Wimbledon	L	39-44
18 June	A	Belle Vue	W	44-40
13 July	H	Harringay	W	54-29
27 July	H	Belle Vue	W	55-29
30 July	A	Harringay	L	24-59
24 August	H	Wembley	W	45-39
25 August	A	Wembley	W	48-35
30 August	A	West Ham	D	42-42
31 August	H	West Ham	W	50-34
7 September	H	Bristol	W	48-34
9 September	A	Bristol	L	31-52
21 September	H	Wimbledon	L	39-45
1 October	A	Harringay	L	32-52
10 October	A	Wimbledon	L	39-43

P24 W15 D1 L8

For 1,072 points; Against 925 points
Finished 1st (out of 7)
National League Division One Champions

1938 – ACU Cup Pool One

7 June	A	West Ham	L	47-61
8 June	H	Harringay	W	75-32
15 June	H	West Ham	D	54-54
25 June	A	Harringay	L	51-57

Finished 2nd in pool
Did not qualify for final

1938 – National Trophy

First round

| 6 July | H | Wimbledon | L | 50-57 |
| 11 July | A | Wimbledon | L | 46-62 |

Lost 96-119 on aggregate

1938 – London Cup

First round

Bye

Semi-final

13 September	A	West Ham	L	52–56
14 September	H	West Ham	W	62–46

Won 114–102 on aggregate

Final

3 October	H	Wimbledon	W	55–52
19 October	A	Wimbledon	L	49–57

Lost 104–109 on aggregate

1938 – National League Division One Averages

Rider	M	R	Pts	BP	T	CMA	FM	PM
Jack Milne	24	96	257	6	263	10.96	12	2
George Newton	23	91	186	4	190	8.35	3	0
Ron Johnson	24	93	156	27	183	7.87	0	2
Stan Greatrex	23	89	140	7	147	6.61	0	0
Bill Longley	24	80	1098	21	129	6.45	1	1
Clem Mitchell	23	88	112	22	134	6.09	0	1
Goldy Restall	11	38	39	9	48	5.05	0	0
Joe Francis	14	41	36	6	42	4.10	0	0
Ernie Evans	19	42	32	10	42	4.00	0	0

1939

Before the 1939 season, the New Cross management made themselves busy with new improvements, both for the riders and for the supporters. Firstly, they relaid the track, as well as laying down an entirely smooth tarmac starting line following instructions from the Control Board. Secondly, they built a new stand with more comfortable accommodation, while away from the stadium they arranged with Southern Railway for a special combined rail and admission ticket at a substantial reduction, the first team in the country to make such an arrangement.

Mockford and Smith were also busy looking for junior talent and, following the closure of New Cross's training school at High Beech, they turned their attentions to Dagenham, which had run two teams in the ill-fated 1938 Sunday Amateur Dirt Track League but had almost closed due to falling crowds. Over the winter, New Cross agreed to 'adopt' the track and keep it open, as long as they could have first pick of the juniors that came up through its ranks.

Once again it was announced that New Cross would start the British season, with their first meeting on 29 March. They were hopeful that they could keep the same team together, although it was now becoming more and more apparent that Newton would not be able to start the season, if indeed he would ever be able to ride again. Also, the Control Board threw a spanner in the works by announcing it was reconsidering the position of foreign riders, especially the Americans. And then, just before the start of the season, Clem Mitchell wrote to New Cross from Australia, saying that he had been off-colour during the winter and his riding was well below par. He felt it would not be worthwhile for him to return to the team, so he had decided to stay in Australia. Mockford and Smith hoped this was just a temporary phase and were still trying to make their minds up whether to ask him to come back when the season began.

Just before the opening meeting it was announced that Newton would miss the whole of the season on his doctor's advice. There was talk of a 'complete recovery' by June, but a rest for the whole of the season would see him back fitter than ever for the 1940 season. Fortunately, the Control Board agreed that the Americans could return, with Jack Milne continuing at New Cross. However, there was a big 'if' and that was that if Newton or Mitchell returned, New Cross would have to give up one of their riders to accommodate him.

Having finally decided not to ask Mitchell back, the New Cross team was announced as Greatrex (captain), Johnson, Francis, Milne. Newton, Longley, Evans, Restall, Ray Duggan, Bill Clibbett and juniors Norman Wolsey, Ken Blair and Alex Gray. With so many juniors fighting for a place, New Cross put on a team trial match. Longley, who had returned from a good winter out in Australia, proved to be the best rider on show, with Johnson, Greatrex and Francis all showing good form. Of the younger riders, Ray Duggan, brother of the more illustrious Vic, showed that he had what it took to force his way into the team proper.

A new competition was introduced that year, the British Speedway Cup. This was run on a league basis with all the National League teams taking part, except Wembley but including Southampton, who had taken over Bristol's licence. This new competition tried out a new point-scoring system with home teams gaining two points for a win and one for a draw as normal, but away teams scoring three points for a win and two points for a draw.

New Cross's first official fixture of the season was in this new league on 12 April against Harringay. The result was a 45-45 draw, which under the new rules meant that New Cross got one point and Harringay two.

Milne was in good form in the Rangers' first away match of the season at Belle Vue, scoring 14 out of a possible 15 points, but his only real support came from the experienced Francis, with Evans popping up at reserve and scoring six points from three rides, as New Cross went down 58-38.

Another big defeat followed, this time at West Ham, who won 60-36 and it was obvious to all that the New Cross team of 1939 was not the same as the one that had carried all before them in the 1938 league season. They were missing Newton, especially, and there was no one yet capable of making up for the loss of his scoring power.

Looking to strengthen the team, Mockford signed up the Canadian Emerson 'Crocky' Rawding, but not without a bit of a rumpus. After Mockford announced the signing, Wembley claimed that Rawding had been on their retained list for two months while Southampton argued that as they were the weakest team in the league, he should go to them. However, Mockford fought tooth and nail to keep his new signing, while Rawding himself said he wanted to ride for New Cross. As it happened, his first match in the Rangers' orange and black was against Southampton and, although he only scored one point, he was part of a rejuvenated New Cross team which trounced the South Coast side 68-28.

Sadly, their much improved home form seemed to desert the Rangers when they travelled away, as they lost their next two matches at Harringay and Wimbledon in the British Speedway Cup by the identical score of 37-58, thus putting paid to any chance they may have had of taking the cup.

With the end of the British Speedway Cup, the National League season started. And it was an unmitigated disaster. The first match, away at West Ham, was lost 33–50. Then followed two home matches, against West Ham and Wimbledon, both of which were lost as well. They then had the misfortune to have a run of five away matches between 25 May and 17 June, all of which they lost without once ever really coming close to taking the points.

In spite of this appalling league record, New Cross took the first step towards regaining the London Cup by bundling out West Ham in the first round. After losing 50–56 in the first leg at Custom House, the Rangers rallied round the following evening to record their first win since 10 May, beating the Hammers 57–50, winning on aggregate by a single point, 107-106.

Nevertheless, apart from this one win, New Cross had shown themselves to be just about the weakest team in the league and so, when the Wembley star Frank Charles decided on a comeback after a short retirement, Mockford immediately slapped in a request to the Control Board that he should be allocated to New Cross and not return to Wembley. Failing that, New Cross should be allocated Morian Hansen, the rider Wembley had brought into replace Charles. The Control Board, however, would have none of it and Charles returned to Wembley to ride alongside Hansen.

As the Rangers went into their next league match on 21 June – at home to Wembley of all teams – they had the unenviable record of having ridden eight league matches and lost the lot. With great irony, the result of the match came down to a last-heat decider with the scores standing at New Cross 39, Wembley 38, with Charles and Hansen out as the two Wembley riders. Up against them were Longley and Duggan. On present form, it seemed almost certain that New Cross were about to lose their ninth match in a row. It seemed even more certain when Duggan reared as the tapes went up and was knocked out, leaving just Longley to face the Wembley pair in the rerun. At the second time of asking, Hansen got a clear lead, followed by Longley and Charles in that order, which remained the same for three-and-a-half laps. But, suddenly, and for no apparent reason, half a lap from home, Hansen fell, Leaving Longley to come home in front of Charles, scoring a 3-2 and giving New Cross the match by two points, 42-40. And so, at the ninth attempt, the league champions won a match in the league.

With just one win in the league, New Cross now faced Harringay in the first round of the National Trophy. no one gave the Rangers much of a chance but they confounded the critics by winning the first leg at Harringay by two points. The turnaround in fortune was largely due to reserve Ray Duggan, who scored nine points from his four rides, although it was Greatrex's heroic long push for home in Heat 17 to gain two points after his motor had packed up that finally made the difference.

It was a good win, but given their recent record, two points was certainly not a big enough lead to guarantee the Rangers passage through to the semi-finals, even though the second leg was at home. But New Cross got off to a great start with a 5-1 in the first heat from Greatrex and Restall and, although Harringay fought back, it was once again Duggan who helped win the match with a 10 paid 11 haul to back up Milne's 18-point maximum and give the Rangers a 57-51 win on the night and a 111-103 victory overall.

Buoyed up by the success of their National Trophy first-round matches, New Cross then experienced the rare sensation of winning a league match as they scraped home against West Ham by just three points. Going into the final heat the scores were New Cross 40 West Ham 37. Out in the final heat for New Cross were Duggan and Restall and for West Ham, Eric Chitty and Charlie Spinks. For the third match running, it was Duggan who made the difference between winning and losing. He had already scored six points from three rides and he shot out of the gate, rode with all the coolness of a veteran, and came home first for the three points needed to win the match, with the final score being New Cross 43, West Ham 40.

Then, in a sensational match at Wimbledon, the Rangers managed to pull off their first away victory of the season. At the end of an incredibly exciting match, Duggan and Rawding went out for New Cross, needing a 4-2 to win the match and they did just that, as Duggan – who just twenty minutes earlier had been carried off the track on a stretcher following a bad crash – took first place from former New Cross man, Nobby Key, but it was Rawding's all-important third place that gave the Rangers victory by 42 points to 41.

New Cross's next home fixture was the long-awaited National Trophy semi-final first leg against Belle Vue. The National Trophy was now the team's last hope of any honours in 1939 but the home leg finished off any chance they may have had as the Rangers lost 64-44, leaving them to make up a deficit of 20 points in Manchester. The difference between the two teams lay mainly in their starting. In almost every heat, the Belle Vue riders were away like lightning, leaving the New Cross boys to play catch-up. And only Milne ever did, apart from one classic race in which Duggan caught and passed both his opponents, Frank Varey and Jack Hargreaves.

With no hope of qualifying for the final, the New Cross riders just seemed to give up in the second leg and lost to Belle Vue by a National Trophy record score of 28-80. The final aggregate score of Belle Vue 144, New Cross 72 meant that all the Rangers had to look forward to now was completing the National League season and, so far were they behind in that, there seemed no chance of them getting themselves out of the cellar position.

Two New Cross riders qualified for the World Championship final, Milne, in joint-seventh place, carrying over six bonus points, and Johnson, in joint-eleventh place with five bonus points. Top of the qualifying list was Jack's brother, Cordy, with eight bonus points. Before the final, there was another match for New Cross to race, a home National League match against Harringay on 30 August. Sadly, this resulted in yet another home defeat as the Rangers were overwhelmed 50-34.

As it happened this was the last National League match to be raced anywhere in the country for seven years as, when war was declared on 3 September, speedway racing was suspended immediately, which also meant that the 1939 World Championship final was never held. For New Cross, the 1939 season had been a catastrophe: from league champions to bottom of the league in one season. If speedway had continued in 1940, Mockford would have needed to have made some drastic changes, but, as it was, there was to be no more speedway at New Cross until 1945 and no more league speedway until 1946.

1939 – National League Division One

16 May	A	West Ham	L	33-50
17 May	H	West Ham	L	41-42
24 May	H	Wimbledon	L	38-45
25 May	A	Wembley	L	31-52
29 May	A	Southampton	L	35-48
5 June	A	Wimbledon	L	32-52
10 June	A	Harringay	L	40-43
17 June	A	Belle Vue	L	30-54
21 June	H	Wembley	W	42-40
28 June	H	Belle Vue	D	42-42
18 July	A	West Ham	L	38-45
19 July	H	Wimbledon	L	35-49
2 August	H	West Ham	W	43-40
5 August	A	Belle Vue	L	27-56
9 August	H	Southampton	W	56-28
10 August	A	Wembley	L	24-59
12 August	A	Southampton	L	32.5-51.5
14 August	A	Wimbledon	W	42-41
30 August	H	Harringay	L	34-50

P19 W4 D1 L14

For 695.5 points; Against 887.5 points

New Cross were 7th out of 7 teams on the suspension of speedway at the outbreak of the Second World War

1939 – British Speedway Cup

10 April	A	Southampton	W	58-38
12 April	H	Harringay	D	47-47
18 April	A	West Ham	L	36-60
19 April	H	West Ham	W	60-36
22 April	A	Belle Vue	L	58-38
26 April	H	Wimbledon	W	59-37
3 May	H	Southampton	W	68-28
6 May	A	Harringay	L	37-58
8 May	A	Wimbledon	L	37-58
10 May	H	Belle Vue	W	51-43

P10 W5 D1 L4
For 491 points; Against 463 points
Finished 4th (out of 6)

1939 – National Trophy

First round

| 22 July | A | Harringay | W | 54-52 |
| 26 July | H | Harringay | W | 57-51 |

Won 111-103 on aggregate

Semi-final

| 16 August | H | Belle Vue | L | 44-64 |
| 26 August | A | Belle Vue | L | 28-80 |

Lost 144-72 on aggregate

1939 – London Cup

First round

Bye

Semi-final

| 13 June | A | West Ham | L | 50-56 |
| 14 June | H | West Ham | W | 57-50 |

Won 107-106 on aggregate

Final

| 5 July | H | Wimbledon | L | 46-62 |
| 10 July | A | Wimbledon | L | 36-72 |

Lost 82-134 on aggregate

1939 – National League Division One Averages

Rider	M	R	Pts	BP	T	CMA	FM	PM
Jack Milne	19	76	189	1	190	10.00	6	0
Ron Johnson	19	76	150.5	1	151.5	7.97	0	0
Stan Greatrex	19	76	113	6	119	6.26	0	0
Ray Duggan	19	64	67	12	79	4.94	0	0
Norman Evans	9	23	21	7	28	4.87	0	0
Bill Longley	19	71	59	19	78	4.39	0	0
Goldy Restall	19	73	56	14	70	3.84	0	0
Joe Francis	17	51	33	11	44	3.45	0	0

three

Post-War at
New Cross

1946

Only Belle Vue and, to a lesser extent, Rye House, had kept going through the war years. New Cross riders Johnson, Longley and Norman Evans had all managed to put in some appearances at Belle Vue, with Bill Longley winning the 1942 Belle Vue Speedway Derby and Johnson proving victorious in the All England Best Pairs Trophy with Alec Statham in 1945.

New Cross was one of the first tracks to get back to action when the war finished and was able to run a limited season of opening meetings in 1945; the biggest meeting was the first running of the London Riders' Championship since 1939 and it was won, fittingly, by Ron Johnson.

League speedway recommenced in 1946 with two leagues, the National League and the Northern League. The Rangers once again took their place with the elite clubs in the National League, along with Belle Vue, Bradford, Wembley, West Ham and Wimbledon. Because there had been no league speedway for six years, the Speedway Control Board pooled and graded all the riders into five different grades. The teams then had to take it in turns to choose a rider from the pool, with the proviso that only one grade-one rider was allowed per team. The draw took place on 7 March and the teams were put into a hat with the first one out being allowed the first pick. As it happened, New Cross were first out and immediately chose the man who had been with the Crystal Palace/New Cross promotion since 1928, Ron Johnson. By the time it came to the seventh and final pick, Mockford was left with a number of juniors and eventually plumped for Irish-born Eric French. French had been a reserve with Wimbledon in 1939 and was in and out of the team without showing any real form, but Mockford decided to choose him on the grounds that: 'he was a decent, clean-living sort of lad who seemed the type that would try.' Mockford decided to hand him over to Alf Cole, formerly Tom Farndon and George Newton's trainer, for a bit of coaching. Within a fortnight, French's best time for four

A scene from the first post-war meeting at New Cross on 27 June 1945.

laps of New Cross had dropped by four seconds and he looked like being the find of the year. Along with Johnson and French, the rest of the team chosen from the draw was Les Wotton, Phil Bishop, Geoff Pymar, Mick Mitchell and Jack Cooley.

New Cross's first two league matches of the season were home and away ties against West Ham on consecutive nights. The Rangers got off to a great start as they won both of them, 43-41 away and 46-36 at home. Johnson scored a maximum in each match. The great start to the season came to an abrupt end as they lost at home, 41-43, to Bradford in their third match, even though Johnson scored his third successive maximum. With Phil Bishop missing this match, a new rider was brought into the team, the veteran South African, Keith Harvey.

After this slight setback, New Cross returned to winning ways with a home victory over Belle Vue 46-37, Johnson scoring his fourth successive maximum. They then travelled up to Manchester and destroyed Belle Vue on their own track, 55-29. Johnson missed out on his fifth consecutive maximum as he dropped a point to Wally Lloyd.

One more victory, a narrow one, 42-41, at home to Wimbledon followed and then it all seemed to go wrong. After the match against Wimbledon on 15 May, New Cross were top of the league, looking as though they would be the first post-war National League champions, but there then followed a run of six matches without a victory, including two at home. The main reason for this was firstly that Bishop missed all of these matches through a muscle injury and secondly — and more importantly — Johnson suffered a broken rib in a fall at Wimbledon. Although he still managed to ride in all six matches, his form slumped dramatically.

In fact, so well had Johnson been riding at the start of the season that he had been nominated as the first challenger for the revived British Match Race Championship, which had been restored to the calendar after eleven years following Tom Farndon's death. Wembley's Bill Kitchen had been nominated as the first champion with Johnson the first challenger. The first leg took place at Wembley on 9 May, with Johnson scoring a stunning 2-0 victory and seemingly headed for the title, but back home at New Cross, a very disappointed crowd saw him fall twice. The decider was held at Wimbledon. Once again in the first leg, Johnson fell, crashing heavily into the safety fence with his machine falling on top of him. The ambulance men spent some time with him, strapping up his side. In spite of this, Johnson agreed to go out for the second run. By the end of the first lap, Johnson held a small lead but on the first bend of the second lap, Kitchen cut inside him causing him to wobble and fall yet again. The New Cross supporters were once again dismayed, but when the announcer revealed that Johnson had, in fact, ridden the second leg with two broken ribs, there was tumultuous cheering in the stadium.

As before the war, Mockford and Smith were keen to train up youngsters, but this time, instead of using training tracks like High Beech or Dagenham, they decided to use their own track and held a ten-week course. Smith gave lectures on the New Cross set-up and general information about being a speedway rider, there were practical lessons on how to ride the track given by Johnson, while Alf Cole and Johnson combined to give demonstrations with Johnson making deliberate mistakes and Cole asking the youngsters what he had done wrong.

Although the Rangers were losing all their league matches, they were having a bit more luck in other competitions as they won their first three matches in the ACU Cup and also beat Wimbledon, 59-49, in the home leg of their London Cup semi-final. However, Wimbledon won the second leg 60-46 to go through 109-105 on aggregate. New Cross's interest in the National Trophy came to an end in the first round as they lost both legs to Belle Vue, going out 115-99 on aggregate.

The Rangers' losing run in the league came to an end on 27 July as they beat Bradford at home, 45-39. Johnson was beginning to come back to the form he had shown at the start of the season and scored a maximum in this match. However, just as he returned, Wotton was injured and he missed several matches. Jack Cooley was dropped from the team after a string of six consecutive zero scores. Their places in the team were taken by Frank Lawrence and Ray Moore. Lawrence had been a junior at Dagenham in 1939 but on the resumption of speedway had joined West Ham, from whom he was transferred in exchange for Cooley. Lawrence had been a fighter pilot at the beginning of the war, but was shot down and spent four years in a prisoner-of-war camp. His continual never-say-die efforts earned him the nickname 'Tiger'. Moore was a Rye House junior who Mockford had spotted and signed up for the team. Both were brought in before they were really ready for top-grade racing, but with Wotton and Bishop both injured, Mockford had little choice.

Eric French, stalwart of the immediate post-war team, rode for New Cross from 1946 to 1953 and was captain for the last three years.

Following the victory over Bradford, New Cross did not win another league match for the rest of the season, losing seven on the trot. Although Wotton returned, Johnson was injured again and missed the last three.

After a very promising start, the New Cross season just got worse and worse and they finished second from bottom of the table. There were some bright spots, however, in particular the form of Ron Johnson. Johnson was now in the veteran stages of his career but had never ridden better. As well as challenging for the Match Race title, Johnson also qualified for the final of the British Riders' Championship, the immediate post-war equivalent of the world championship, finishing in ninth place with seven points. He may well have done better but suffered a bad crash the night before. And, in spite of struggling with his fractured rib for part of the season, he still managed to finish the year with a cma of 10.69, fourth best in the league and his best ever, scoring nine full maximums on the way. He also followed in the tradition of Farndon and Milne by winning the London Riders' Championship for the second time.

The other bright spot was the continuing improvement of Eric French. In the last meeting of the season at home to Wimbledon he returned his first double-points score, with ten points, to be New Cross's top scorer. Frank Lawrence also showed flashes of talent towards the end so there was hope that it might be a very different story in 1947.

One other bright spot was, that in spite of the poor performance of the team for most of the year, New Cross was attracting record crowds. The capacity was 30,000 and on a number of occasions the gates had to be closed as there was no more room inside.

1946 – National League Division One

23 April	A	West Ham	W	43–41
24 April	H	West Ham	W	46–36
1 May	H	Bradford	L	41–43
8 May	H	Belle Vue	W	46–37
11 May	A	Belle Vue	W	55–29
15 May	H	Wimbledon	W	42–41
18 May	A	Bradford	L	23–54
22 May	H	Wembley	L	36–48
23 May	A	Wembley	L	24–54
27 May	A	Wimbledon	L	40–41
18 June	A	West Ham	D	42–42
17 July	H	West Ham	L	38–46
24 July	H	Bradford	W	45–39
27 July	A	Bradford	L	39–45
4 September	H	Wembley	L	37–46
5 September	A	Wembley	L	30–53
14 September	A	Belle Vue	L	28–56
18 September	H	Belle Vue	L	30–53
23 September	A	Wimbledon	L	25–59
25 September	H	Wimbledon	L	39–45

P20 W6 D1 L13
For 749 points; Against 908 points
Finished 5th (out of 6)

1946 – National Trophy

First round

8 June	A	Belle Vue	L	49–58
12 June	H	Belle Vue	L	50–57

Lost 99–115 on aggregate

1946 – London Cup

Semi-final

| 26 June | H | Wimbledon | W | 59-49 |
| 8 July | A | Wimbledon | L | 46-60 |

Lost 105-109 on aggregate

1946 – ACU Cup

League phase

5 June	H	Wimbledon	W	54-40
10 June	A	Wimbledon	W	50-45
3 July	H	Belle Vue	W	49-47
4 July	A	Wembley	L	37-57
3 August	A	Belle Vue	L	38-57
6 August	A	West Ham	W	54-42
8 August	H	West Ham	W	61-35
14 August	H	Wembley	L	39-55
24 August	A	Bradford	L	46-50
28 August	H	Bradford	W	50-46

P10 W6 D0 L4 Pts 14

For 478 points; Against 474 points

Finished 3rd (out of 6). Did not qualify for final.

1946 – National League Division One Averages

Rider	M	R	Pts	BP	T	CMA	FM	PM
Ron Johnson	17	67	179	0	179	10.69	9	0
Geoff Pymar	19	76	164	0	164	8.63	0	0
Les Wotton	17	68	136	4	140	8.24	0	0
Eric French	19	75	99	12	111	5.92	0	0
Mick Mitchell	19	69	55	17	72	4.17	0	0
Phil Bishop	11	29	24	6	40	4.14	0	0
Frank Lawrence	9	36	30	4	34	3.78	0	0
Keith Harvey	16	40	25	9	34	3.40	0	0
Ray Moore	9	28	12	4	16	2.29	0	0
Jack Cooley	11	31	12	5	17	2.19	0	0

1947

The popularity of speedway had grown so quickly that ten more teams applied to join the league set-up in 1947. The Control Board decided to abandon the Northern League and to create three divisions of the National League. New Cross were in the first division, along with Belle Vue, Bradford, Harringay, Wembley, West Ham and Wimbledon.

Mockford announced that the team would consist of Johnson, Wotton, Pymar, French, Lawrence, Mitchell, Moore and Harvey from the previous year's team, and a new signing, a young Australian by the name of Ern Brecknell.

New Cross's opening match was a challenge away at Wimbledon on Good Friday. Although the Rangers lost, both Johnson and French showed good form, scoring 12 and nine points respectively. Later the same day, Johnson and French won a best pairs event at Harringay, with Johnson, in a class of his own, once again going through the card unbeaten. Johnson completed a hat-trick of maximums the following week as he scored another 12 points in the home leg of the challenge against Wimbledon.

Before the league season started, a three-way swap brought a pre-war Rangers favourite back home, as Bill Longley was transferred from Bradford to New Cross as part of a deal which took Les Wotton to Wimbledon and Oliver Hart to Bradford.

The first home league match resulted in a good win for the Rangers as they defeated West Ham 47-37, with Johnson, 11, French, 10, and Longley, 10, all scoring double figures. Sadly, however, the victory was a bit of a one-off as the Rangers proceeded to lose nine of their next 11 matches. During this run, Mockford and Smith made a number of attempts to strengthen the team. Harvey was dropped and his place taken by a young Australian called Ken Le Breton, but after just two matches he was on his way to Newcastle in exchange (plus £1,000) for their star rider, Jeff Lloyd. Following his tremendous early season form for second division Newcastle, Lloyd had been the

Eric French in action leading Belle Vue's Louis Lawson.

subject of great interest from at least three other London clubs, Wembley, Wimbledon and Harringay, who had all been after his signature, but it was Cecil Smith, on behalf of New Cross, who finally got him to sign up.

The other newcomer to arrive at New Cross raised some eyebrows as Mockford and Smith welcomed the 1936 world champion, Lionel Van Praag, to the side. To make way for Van Praag, Mitchell was dropped and loaned out to second division Birmingham.

New Cross took a rest from National League action as a new competition, the British Speedway Cup, was introduced. This was run on a league basis, with each team meeting once each home and away. Although Wembley proved to be invincible, winning every single match, New Cross finished as runners-up, wining eight out of 12 matches.

Also during this period, the first round of the London Cup was held with the Rangers beating Wimbledon 64-44 at home and 55-52 away. Longley was the hero of both legs, scoring 16 and 15 respectively, but really the New Cross line-up was becoming a very potent one with five top liners plus Eric French, who could normally be relied on to add five or six to the total. In addition, the two regular reserves, Lawrence and Moore, were also performing well in their reserves races. Such was the form of Johnson, Longley and Van Praag that they were chosen for Australia in all three Test matches that year, while Lloyd was picked at reserve in the last Test for England.

New Cross suffered their first major setback for a while when they took on Belle Vue in the National Trophy first round. Going down by 26 points, 41-67, at Belle Vue, they were unable to pick up sufficient points back at the Old Kent Road to make it through to the second round. A score of 61-46 saw them go out on aggregate, 113-102.

Nevertheless, their good league form continued and they won three of their next four matches losing just once, to the all-conquering Wembley Lions, 39-45. Although there was no chance of picking up league honours, there was still hope of picking up a trophy as New Cross had always done well in the London Cup. They now faced a semi-final match against Harringay. The first leg was at Harringay and resulted in the best away win of the season for any team in any competition as the Rangers trounced Harringay 72-36. New Cross won the second leg by an even bigger margin, 74-34, going through with the mammoth total of 146 to Harringay's miserable 70.

The Rangers were now through to the final, where they would be up against Wembley, runaway winners of the National League and the British Speedway Cup. Not only that, but Wembley had already beaten New Cross at the Frying Pan twice that year. Although the Rangers were now a force to be reckoned with, it nevertheless looked a hopeless task that faced them. And, indeed, that is just how it looked as Wembley took the first leg 58-49 at New Cross. Going into the second leg at the Empire Stadium with a nine-point deficit, not even the most passionate of supporters would have given the boys in orange and black much of a chance. Even when Johnson and French pulled off a 5-1 in the first heat it still seemed hopeless, but then Lloyd and Longley followed this up with another 5-1 in Heat 2 and, suddenly, the Rangers were only one point behind. A 4-2 to Wembley in Heat 3 reversed the trend but in Heat 6, Pymar and Lloyd scored a third 5-1 for the visitors. From then on, it was all New Cross as they completely outrode the opposition to pull off an amazing 61-47 victory, giving them the London Cup 110-105 on aggregate. Johnson was on magnificent form, scoring a 15-point maximum.

Unexpected though it was, the title of London champions was a fitting tribute to a team that had started the season so badly but had fought back so brilliantly. Four of the squad qualified for the British Riders' Championship final, more than any other team. Pymar finished in thirteenth place with four points, Johnson in eleventh place with six points and Van Praag fifth with eight points. But the star of the Rangers' contingent was Bill Longley, who stood proudly on the rostrum in third place behind Jack Parker and Bill Kitchen. On his way, he had taken such notable scalps as Kitchen himself, Vic Duggan, Norman Parker, George Wilks and Eric Chitty.

1947 – National League Division One

15 April	A	West Ham	L	37-47
16 April	H	West Ham	W	47-37
23 April	H	Bradford	L	38-45
26 April	A	Bradford	L	38-46
30 April	H	Belle Vue	L	36-46
3 May	A	Belle Vue	L	37-47
7 May	H	Harringay	W	42-41
9 May	A	Harringay	L	40-44

14 May	H	Wembley	L	33-51
15 May	A	Wembley	L	34-50
11 June	H	Harringay	W	52-31
14 June	A	Bradford	L	37-44
16 June	A	Wimbledon	L	33-50
18 June	H	Wimbledon	W	47-37
25 June	H	Belle Vue	W	49-35
28 June	A	Belle Vue	L	34-50
2 July	H	West Ham	W	59-25
1 August	A	Harringay	W	44-39
27 August	H	Wembley	L	39-45
10 September	H	Bradford	W	58-26
22 September	A	Wimbledon	W	45-39
24 September	H	Wimbledon	W	50-34
30 September	A	West Ham	L	39-45
2 October	A	Wembley	L	27-57

P24 W10 D0 L14
For 995 points; Against 1,011 points
Finished 5th (out of 7)

1947 – British Speedway Cup

League phase

19 May	A	Wimbledon	L	43-52
21 May	H	Wimbledon	W	49-46
4 June	H	Wembley	L	45-47
6 June	A	Harringay	W	53-43
3 July	A	Wembley	L	36-60
9 July	H	Bradford	W	64-31
16 July	H	Belle Vue	W	57.5-37.5
19 July	A	Bradford	W	62-34
30 July	H	Harringay	W	63-33
5 August	A	West Ham	W	60-33
27 September	A	Belle Vue	L	40-56
1 October	H	West Ham	W	66-29

P12 W8 D0 L4
For 638.5 points; Against 501.5 points
Finished 2nd (out of 6). Did not qualify for final.

1947 – National Trophy

First round

9 August	A	Belle Vue	L	41-67
13 August	H	Belle Vue	W	61-47

Lost 102-113 on aggregate

1947 – London Cup

First round

23 July	H	Wimbledon	W	64-44
28 July	A	Wimbledon	W	55-52

Won 119-96 on aggregate

Semi-final

20 August	H	Harringay	W	74-34
22 August	A	Harringay	W	72-36

Won 146-70 on aggregate

Final

17 September	H	Wembley	L	49-58
18 September	A	Wembley	W	61-47

Won 110-105 on aggregate

1947 – National League Division One Averages

Rider	M	R	Pts	BP	T	CMA	FM	PM
Ron Johnson	24	96	194	19	213	8.88	1	0
Bill Longley	24	95	185	3	188	7.92	1	0
Lionel Van Praag	13	49	89	7	96	7.84	0	1
Geoff Pymar	24	96	163	22	185	7.71	0	2
Jeff Lloyd	14	56	93	11	104	7.43	0	0
Eric French	24	94	122	18	140	5.96	0	0
Ray Moore	24	66	66	20	86	5.21	0	0
Mick Mitchell	12	40	35	7	42	4.20	0	0
Frank Lawrence	22	57	38	16	54	3.79	0	0

1948

Lionel Van Praag returned home to Australia at the end of the 1947 season, but, apart from his departure, the team announced at the beginning of the 1948 season remained the same. The opening meeting of the season was an individual trophy meeting for the Rangers Plaque. A number of top riders from other tracks took part, including Split Waterman, Tommy Price, Bill Kitchen and Eric Chitty, but it was the New Cross riders who took the first four places with Pymar winning a run-off from Johnson and Lloyd to take the plaque. The surprise fourth-placed rider was reserve, Ray Moore.

However, apart from the brilliant form shown by the New Cross riders there were two other events that made this a very special meeting. The first was the return to the saddle of former New Cross favourite, George Newton, having his first outing in public for nearly ten years. He took it all very slow and steady, but just to see him back amazed all those who knew just how seriously ill he had been. The other event was the filming of crowd scenes for a new film based on a speedway theme called *Once a Jolly Swagman*, starring Dirk Bogarde.

The second home meeting was a challenge match against Wimbledon, which the Rangers won 51-33 to serve notice that they were definitely very much in business. Pymar and Johnson continued their good form, both scoring maximums. In fact, Johnson now seemed to be riding better than at any time in his life. He was forty-one years old, an age at which most speedway riders would consider retiring – if indeed they were still riding – but Johnson just seemed to be getting better and better. In a statement to the Press after the meeting, he said that he intended racing until he was fifty-two. Moore continued the good form he had shown at the opening meeting, scoring nine points, while Newton made his first appearance in a New Cross team for

Frank Lawrence rode for New Cross from 1946 to 1953, but never rose above second-string standard.

ten years. Sadly he did not score any points, though he did show one or two flashes of his old spectacular form.

The first two league matches were home and away encounters against Bradford, both of which the Rangers won, by the big score of 55-28 at home and then 42-40 away. Newton showed a big improvement and scored his first points for the team, with three in each leg, both from two rides. Johnson was continuing to lead the way and was nominated as the first challenger of 1948 for Jack Parker's Match Race title. In what could be seen as a warm-up for this encounter, New Cross took on Parker's Belle Vue team in home and away league matches. Although the match score was 1-1 – Belle Vue winning 53-31 at Hyde Road and New Cross 61-23 at the Old Kent Road – Johnson got the better of Parker on the two occasions they met, finishing with ten points at Belle Vue and yet another maximum at home. But the big cheers were reserved for Newton, who won both his races at New Cross.

Three more victories in the next three matches followed, the first an important win over favourites for the league title, Wembley. By the end of April, New Cross were sitting at the top of the table, having won six out of seven matches, including two away victories.

There was not a weak link in the team. Johnson, Pymar, Longley and Lloyd were all able to match the best in the league, while French, Moore and Lawrence were coming on in leaps and bounds and able to give very strong second-string support, while best of all from the Rangers' point of view, was the form of Newton, who was now getting right back into his stride and generally proving far too much for the other teams' reserves.

A big anniversary meeting was laid on for 19 May, as it marked the twentieth anniversary of the first meeting at Crystal Palace back on 19 May 1928. The main event of the evening was an individual trophy with all the New Cross team and some of the top stars of the day, such as Vic Duggan, Split Waterman, Jack Parker and Eric Chitty. As well as those, Mockford and Smith, who had been in charge at Crystal Palace and New Cross ever since that first meeting, invited all the riders who were still using the old leg-trailing style, including their own George Newton. Fittingly, the winner of the event with a maximum 15 points, was the man who had been with the promotion since day one, Ron Johnson. But it was a close call as, in Heat 19, with Johnson on 12 points and Pymar on 11 and with Duggan already finished on 14 points, one of the most breathtakingly exciting races seen at the Frying Pan since the war took place as Pymar tried everything he knew to get past Johnson. In the end,

Ron Johnson teaching a group of novices at New Cross in 1947.

Johnson took the race and the trophy by inches on the line. In addition to winning the trophy, Johnson was also presented with a brand new bike by Messrs Mockford, Smith and Cole in honour of his contribution to Crystal Palace and New Cross over the twenty years.

The following evening there was, if anything, even more of a celebration, as New Cross beat their main rivals for the National League, Wembley, away. Once again, it was Johnson, now in the form of his life, who ensured victory for the Rangers. Going into the final heat, the score was Wembley 39.5, New Cross 38.5. Out for the Rangers were Johnson, who had already broken the track record in the match, and Moore. As the tapes went up, Moore managed to take the lead with Johnson close behind. From then on, Johnson nursed Moore round, keeping Wembley's star man, Tommy Price, at bay. It was a triumphant Johnson and Moore who came in for a 5-1 and a 43.5-40.5 victory.

New Cross followed up this body blow against Wembley by beating them at home the following week. And then, two nights later, winning away at Harringay. On that occasion, Johnson did not return his usual double-point score, as he fell foul of a new instruction from the Control Board that riders were to be punished if they looked back during a race. He received a warning after the fifth heat and when he repeated the offence in his next outing he was immediately disqualified. The next week saw the London Riders' Championship being held at New Cross with Johnson as the red-hot favourite to regain the title he had won in 1945 and '46, but it was not to be, as Wembley's Split Waterman took the title. Waterman's only loss was at the hands of Johnson, who set a new track record of 57.8 seconds in the race, beating Newton's time of 58 seconds set as far back as 1938. This was the second time Johnson had set the track record, the first being fourteen years previously. Unfortunately for Johnson, however, he fell in his last race, putting him out of the running.

There was a month's break from National League action as the teams fought for a new trophy, the Anniversary Cup. After giving young Australian Lindsay Mitchell a few outings in place of the injured Geoff Pymar, who was suffering from badly torn ligaments in his left knee, New Cross turned to the Division Three Match Race Champion, Exeter's Cyril Roger, and signed him up on a temporary basis. He proved an instant hit, winning his first race against Belle Vue in the Anniversary Cup match on 5 June.

The next big match at New Cross was the third Test match between England and Australia. Four New Cross riders took part in the fixture, with Johnson and Longley turning out for Australia and Lloyd and the much-improved Moore for England. All four acquitted themselves well with Johnson scoring 14 points, Longley ten, Moore seven and Lloyd six. England won the match 57-51. Fred Mockford's announcement at the meeting that from then on rattles would be banned at New Cross was greeted with great applause. He emphasised the great danger connected with these noisy instruments and asked for the co-operation of the crowd.

When National League racing resumed, New Cross were sitting at the top of the table and looked like favourites to win the title. However, the first match after the break came as something of a shock to the system as they were hammered 53-29 at Bradford.

The New Cross National League-winning team of 1948. Back row, left to right: Frank Lawrence, Eric French, Jeff Lloyd, Ron Johnson (captain), Fred Mockford (promoter), Ray Moore, Cyril Roger. Front row: Lindsay Mitchell, Bill Longley.

There was some excuse in the fact that Pymar was still missing, but nevertheless it was hardly a championship performance.

To make matters worse, they lost their next match at Wimbledon and West Ham went to the top of the league. As if things weren't getting bad enough, it was then announced that George Newton had been admitted to hospital suffering from a very rare abdominal complaint and it was not known when he would be fit to return to racing. With Newton out for the foreseeable future, Roger was signed up on a semi-permanent basis. New Cross had another brief respite from the league as they began the defence of their London Cup title with a 65-43 home leg victory over Harringay. This was a much better performance from the team as Johnson and Lloyd each scored 14 points, backed up by Moore and Longley with ten each and French on eight.

This victory seemed to inspire the Rangers and get them back on track in the league. This was complemented by an easy victory over Wimbledon the following week, 58-25. Every single member of the team rode well and, with Pymar back, it looked as though the little hiccup suffered when they lost to Bradford and Wimbledon was now behind them. They continued their fine form by beating Harringay in the London Cup to qualify for the semi-final and then completely swamped Bradford, 77-30, in the first round of the National Trophy.

A still from the film *Once a Jolly Swagman,* some of which was filmed at New Cross.

New Cross then proceeded to beat Wimbledon in the London Cup semi-final, 131–84, after crushing them 80-27 in the home leg. Not only were New Cross winning their matches, they were taking them by large margins. It now looked completely on the cards that they could pull off the treble. The regular team of Johnson, Longley, Pymar, Lloyd, Moore, French, Lawrence and Roger had no equal in British speedway and was turning into one of the most formidable octets ever assembled by one team.

This was re-emphasised in the first leg of the National Trophy semi-final as New Cross completely outrode Birmingham to win by the massive score of 83-25. Although the Rangers did at last lose a match in the second leg of the semi-final, it was not enough to deprive them of their place in the final, so New Cross were now in both finals and in pole position for the league championship.

While the side was dominating the team events, two of them had also made the final of the Riders' Championship (the former British Riders' Championship now renamed because of the increasing number of Australian and North American riders who were back in the country). They were the Australian pair of Johnson and Longley. The final was held on 16 September in front of 90,000 spectators. Johnson met one of the pre-meeting favourites, Wilbur Lamoreaux, in his first ride. As expected, Lamoreaux got away from the gate and led until the fourth bend of the first lap. At this point, Johnson tried an outside overtake on the wet and slippery track, just as Lamoreaux moved across in front of him. The two collided and both went down demolishing several yards of the safety fence in the process. A rerun was ordered with all four riders back as the steward felt no one rider was to blame for the accident. In the rerun, Johnson easily beat Lamoreaux. He lost his next race to Wimbledon's Alec Statham, but then won his third. After losing to eventual winner Vic Duggan in Heat 14, Johnson's final ride was in the last heat. At this stage he had ten points. Duggan had already finished with 14, but behind him was Statham on 13. If Johnson could win his last race, he would be in with a chance of taking the runners-up spot. Up against Oliver Hart, Eric Chitty and Ernie Price, he made no mistake, winning comfortably. Johnson also made no mistake in the run-off to finish as runner-up, thus repeating his 1933 feat when he finished second in the Star Riders' Championship. He received a £100 cheque from the Duke of Edinburgh.

The first trophy up for conclusion was the London Cup. Man for man, Wembley was probably the only team in the country that could match New Cross, with riders such as Wilbur Lamoreaux, Tommy Price, Bill Kitchen, Split Waterman, Freddie Williams and Bill Gilbert. And so it proved as Wembley took a big lead in the first leg, 65–40. Sadly, only Johnson lived up to his reputation, scoring 16 points including a hair-raising final-lap burst to give him victory over Lamoreaux in Heat 5. It was too much to hope that New Cross could make up the 25-point deficit back at the Old Kent Road and although they put up a much better performance, with the young third division recruit Cyril Roger top-scoring with a 15-point maximum, it was not enough and they lost their grip on the London Cup, 98–115.

Back on safer territory in the league, New Cross set about Bradford, beating them 54–30 before moving on to face Wembley yet again, this time in the National Trophy final. Unfortunately for the Rangers, the first leg was pretty much the same story as the London Cup, with Wembley gaining a 20-point advantage. In the return leg, not only did New Cross not make up the deficit, but they even lost 52–56, their first home loss since early May.

Hopes of the treble had evaporated, with both cups being forfeited to Wembley. All that was left now was the league. The position here was that Harringay had now completed all their fixtures and were top of the table with 32 points. West Ham were second, three points behind, with just one match in hand, while New Cross were in third place with 26 points and four matches to race. In effect, New Cross needed to win all four of those matches to take the league title. One of the matches was against West Ham, but the next one was the really vital match as it was away at Wembley, who had just defeated them decisively at the Empire Stadium in their two cup finals.

An advert for *Once a Jolly Swagman*.

The match started with two 4-2s to New Cross, thanks to Johnson and Moore in Heat 1 and Longley and Lawrence in Heat 2. The match swung first one way and then the other, until, with one heat to go, the scores were level at 39-39. It looked all over for the Rangers, as Johnson got away badly from the start, but, in magnificent style, he came from behind to take both Tommy Price and Freddie Williams to win the race. Even better news for the Rangers supporters – who had travelled across London in their thousands to see this vital match – was that Lloyd had sneaked through behind him and was lying in second place. Price managed to overtake him – almost on the line – but a 4-2 was good enough and gave the Rangers a surprise, if very welcome, victory over the team that had deprived them of the treble.

The following evening, New Cross faced their second vital fixture back home at the Frying Pan. It turned into a rout as the Rangers destroyed West Ham 66-18, winning every heat but one and recording 11 5-1s.

The riders were determined not to let another trophy slip from their grasp and, the following evening, they took to the track for their third vital league fixture in three nights as they travelled up to Manchester to take on Belle Vue, the only undefeated home team in the league. But they didn't remain undefeated for long as Johnson, Longley and Lloyd once again led the assault to defeat the Aces 51-33.

There was now just one more match to go to make sure of the league title, a home tie against Belle Vue and the Rangers finished the season in a blaze of glory as they beat the Aces 57-27. Both Longley and Moore scored full maximums while, for the third match running, Pymar and Roger were unbeaten as reserves. It had been a tremendously exciting finish to the league season for New Cross, who had had to win their last four fixtures against tough opposition to take the title. The team received the trophy and cash awards totalling £500 from Mr W. Emsley Carr, vice-chairman of the *News of the World*, at a special ceremony after the match against Belle Vue.

It had been an amazing year for the Rangers. From their poor showing in 1947 and without Lionel Van Praag, New Cross became the team to beat in 1948. They were league champions and finalists in the two major trophies. The driving force behind their success was Ron Johnson, the most experienced rider now active in British speedway, as he had started out in Australia twenty-two years previously in 1926. It was amazing to think that he was now riding better than at any time in his

Geoff Pymar leads his captain, Ron Johnson.

career: he had come second in the Riders' Championship, was second in the league averages and ranked second in the authoritative Stenner's end-of-year rankings. In all cases, he was behind the phenomenal Vic Duggan. Finally, he had continued to be a regular choice for Australia in the Test matches and, in the last match of the series, chalked up his fiftieth appearance, easily a record on both sides. But, of course, he couldn't have transformed New Cross on his own and he had very strong support from the more experienced riders, Jeff Lloyd and Bill Longley, both of whom returned eight-plus averages, and Geoff Pymar. In addition, it was the year the younger element started to come good with both Ray Moore and Eric French scoring at over seven per match and Frank Lawrence at nearly six, while in young Cyril Roger, they had unearthed the find of the season. In his ten matches with the Rangers he scored at an average of 7.27.

1948 – National League Division One

7 April	H	Bradford	W	55–28
10 April	A	Bradford	W	42–40
14 April	H	Belle Vue	W	61–23
17 April	A	Belle Vue	L	31–53
21 April	H	Wembley	W	56–27
26 April	A	Wimbledon	W	44–40
28 April	H	Wimbledon	W	49–35
4 May	A	West Ham	L	35–49
5 May	H	West Ham	W	58–26
12 May	H	Harringay	L	41–43
20 May	A	Wembley	W	43.5–40.5★
26 May	H	Wembley	W	46–38
28 May	A	Harringay	W	47–37
3 July	A	Bradford	L	29–53
19 July	A	Wimbledon	L	38–46
12 August	H	Wimbledon	W	58–25
24 August	A	West Ham	L	35–49
26 August	H	Harringay	W	55–29
30 September	H	Bradford	W	54–30
1 October	A	Harringay	L	40–44
14 October	A	Wembley	W	43–41
15 October	H	West Ham	W	66–18
16 October	A	Belle Vue	W	51–33
22 October	H	Belle Vue	W	57–27

★ Raced at Wimbledon

P24 W17 D0 L7
For 1134.5 points; Against 874.5 points
Finished 1st (out of 7)
New Cross National League Division One Champions

1948 – National Trophy

First round

19 August	H	Bradford	W	77–30
4 September	A	Bradford	L	46–62

Won 123–93 on aggregate

Semi-final

9 September	H	Birmingham	W	83–25
18 September	A	Birmingham	L	69–39

Won 122–94 on aggregate

Final

7 October	A	Wembley	L	44–64
8 October	H	Wembley	L	52–56

Lost 120–96 on aggregate

1948 – London Cup

First round

5 August	H	Harringay	W	65–43
20 August	A	Harringay	L	43–64

Won 108–107 on aggregate

Semi-final

30 August	A	Wimbledon	L	51–57
2 September	H	Wimbledon	W	80–27

Won 131–84 on aggregate

Final

| 23 September | A | Wembley | L | 40–65 |
| 24 September | H | Wembley | W | 58–50 |

Lost 98–115 on aggregate

1948 – Anniversary Cup

15 May	A	Bradford	L	47–48
31 May	A	Wimbledon	W	53–42
5 June	A	Belle Vue	L	42–50
8 June	A	West Ham	L	34–62
9 June	H	West Ham	W	58–38
16 June	H	Bradford	W	51–44
23 June	H	Wembley	W	49–46
24 June	A	Wembley	L	49–47
8 July	H	Harringay	W	49–47
9 July	A	Harringay	L	47–49
15 July	H	Belle Vue	W	57–39
22 July	H	Wimbledon	L	42–54

P12 W6 D0 L6

For 578; Against 566

Finished 4th (out of 7)

1948 – National League Division One Averages

Rider	M	R	Pts	BP	T	CMA	FM	PM
Ron Johnson	24	96	239	11	250	10.42	5	2
Jeff Lloyd	24	96	170	26	196	8.17	0	3
Bill Longley	24	95	171	19	190	8.00	1	1
Geoff Pymar	21	70	116.5	13	129.5	7.40	1	0
Ray Moore	24	93	155	15	170	7.31	2	0
Cyril Roger	10	22	32	8	40	7.27	0	0
Eric French	24	95	133	36	169	7.12	0	1
Frank Lawrence	24	68	80	18	98	5.76	0	0
George Newton	12	27	35	2	37	5.48	0	0

1949

Over the winter, Mockford and Smith stripped the cinder track to its foundations and completely relaid it to give an even better racing surface. New Cross was already considered to have one of the best racing surfaces in the country, but, after seeing the new track, pundits were already declaring it *the* best in speedway.

With the new wave of young riders proving so effective, Pymar decided it was time he moved on and was transferred to Harringay over the close season. Longley also asked for a transfer but eventually came to terms with the New Cross management and signed up for 1949. George Newton declared himself fit for the new season but, sadly, there was no room for the old Rangers favourite and he moved on to Fleetwood.

One addition to the team came in the form of Cyril Roger's brother, Bert, who was said to be at least as good a prospect as his brother, if not better. Bert was originally a road racer and finished eleventh in the 1947 Isle of Man Junior TT. In 1948, when his brother began to make a name for himself in speedway, Bert asked Mockford if he could try out as well. Mockford immediately saw his potential and signed him up, loaning him out to third division Exeter to gain more experience. Although only in his first year as a speedway rider, he topped the Exeter points chart with an average of 9.74, and Mockford recalled him to the New Cross side for the 1949 season.

New Cross's first league match of the season resulted in a victory over West Ham. Bert Roger astounded everyone by beating West Ham's star rider, Aub Lawson, who was ranked No.4 in the world. He also won his other race for a debut reserves' maximum. Following this meeting, the Control Board announced that Johnson would be the first challenger of 1949 for Jack Parker's Match Race title.

At the Good Friday meeting, four Swedish riders, Evert Fransson, Thord Larsson, Stig Pramberg and a young nineteen-year-old junior, Olle Nygren, took part in the second half. Nygren, in particular, showed good form, winning his heat and the final of the International Scratch Race.

It was soon Birmingham's turn to feel the full force of the Rangers' onslaught, going down 56-28. At this stage of the season, things were looking very good for New Cross and they looked well set to repeat their 1948 performance. An added bonus was the poor form of Wembley, who, at this stage of the season, had won just one match out of six.

A special meeting was held on 20 May to celebrate the twenty-first anniversary of Crystal Palace/New Cross with a number of former riders presented to the crowd including ex-captains Roger Frogley and Triss Sharp. Many long time supporters in the crowd reflected on the fact that Frogley and Sharp already seemed like names from the distant past and yet their current top rider, Ron Johnson, had not only also taken part in the very first meeting at Crystal Palace on 19 May 1928, but had even then been the star rider.

A big home victory followed on 27 May as New Cross took Belle Vue apart, winning 51-33, and then three nights later they followed this up with a big win away at Wimbledon, with Cyril Roger scoring a paid maximum and French adding 11 points. The next home match against Wembley took place under the glare of the television cameras as the BBC came to film the match. This time, New Cross made no mistake against the Lions, scoring a convincing 48-36 win with Johnson top-scoring with a paid maximum. Once again French had an excellent meeting, contributing nine from three completed rides.

The following evening, the Rangers were desperately unlucky to lose 41-42 away at Bradford, the home team's victory coming in the last heat. It was a minor irritation, but New Cross soon picked themselves up and won the next three league matches, including a mammoth 64-20 win over Bradford.

After this run, New Cross were at the top of the table, two points in front of Belle Vue with a match in hand. The prospect of retaining their title was looking good. The only slight worry was Wembley, who had recovered from their bad start and were now seven points behind, but with five matches in hand. Nevertheless, the New Cross faithful felt confident as they had the points in the bag and Wembley still had their matches to win.

The next match, therefore, was vital, as it saw New Cross travel to the Empire Stadium to take on the Lions. Sadly, Johnson fell in the first heat and was unable to take part in the rest of the meeting as the fall had aggravated an old thigh injury. As well as this being a blow in itself, his accident seemed to unsettle the rest of the team, who did not ride at their best, handing victory to Wembley by 53 points to 31.

Although this was a blow to New Cross's hopes, the league nevertheless now seemed a two-horse race between New Cross and Wembley, who were continuing their climb up the table. There was no weak link in the New Cross team and all eight riders were proving themselves very effective. But disaster was just around the corner. In the first-round second-leg London Cup match against Wimbledon on 1 August, Heat 7 saw Johnson and Cyril Roger out against Cyril Brine and Alec Statham. Roger and Johnson took the lead from the tapes, but as they rounded the third and fourth bends, Johnson suddenly lost

Mr New Cross himself, Ron Johnson. He was instrumental in bringing speedway to Crystal Palace in 1928, riding in the first-ever meeting, and remained associated with the Crystal Palace/New Cross club until the final season in 1963.

control and was thrown from his machine. Brine, just a few yards behind had no chance to avoid him. There was a deathly hush in the stadium as Johnson made no attempt to move. The track doctor made an immediate examination and Johnson was stretchered off the track. The announcer told the crowd: 'Ron Johnson has been removed to hospital with head injuries which must be considered serious.' It was later reported that Johnson had fractured his skull and would miss the rest of the season. For the record, New Cross won the London Cup tie 113–101 on aggregate.

As if Johnson's injury wasn't bad enough, two weeks later, riding in his first Test match as a full England rider, French crashed and broke his collarbone, putting him out for several weeks. Mockford was forced to bring in two junior riders, Don Gray and Ray Ellis, to take their places and the two injuries more or less finished any chance New Cross had of competing for honours in 1949.

Fortunately, New Cross did have a brief respite from the league as their next two matches were the home and away legs of the National Trophy second round. Even better was that it was against second division opposition in Bristol. Even so, they only managed to pull off a narrow 55-53 victory at the Old Kent Road, thanks mainly to Gray's six points from two rides. It looked almost certain that they would be beaten on aggregate. There was some good news in another way, however, and that was that Mockford was able to announce to the crowd that Johnson was progressing well and was now sitting up and 'taking nourishment'.

With the prospect of a 'giant-killing', 22,000 supporters turned up at Bristol's Knowle Stadium to see the return leg. In spite of the injuries, however, New Cross got off to a brilliant start, with Bert Roger and Longley scoring a 5-1 in the first heat, and Lloyd and Lawrence adding another 5-1 in the second. Bristol never recovered from this and the Rangers went on to win by the somewhat unexpectedly large margin of 60-47.

The following week Cyril Roger was the hero of the side as he scored ten points and also broke the one-lap flying-start record, which had stood since 1937, on the second lap of Heat 5 when he recorded 13.6 seconds. With good support from Moore and Longley, New Cross beat Belle Vue 46-38. In the second half of the meeting, the Rangers met another Swedish team, headed by Olle Nygren, in a four-heat friendly. The New Cross team proved far too experienced for their Swedish opponents and ran out 18-6 victors. Nygren was once again the most impressive Swedish rider on show.

French attempted a comeback in the friendly against the Swedish side but it only served to show that his shoulder was not yet strong enough to hold his machine on the bends and he decided to opt out for a bit longer and take a course of electrical massage treatment. Johnson, meanwhile, had been discharged from hospital and was able to walk short distances.

The victory over Belle Vue was the last victory the Rangers were to experience for another six league matches. The loss of Johnson and French was proving too much for them and, although the two juniors had started reasonably well, they found themselves to be no match for the more experienced reserves in the other teams. After three point-less matches, Ellis was dropped and Bob Baker recalled from his loan at Hull to take up the No.7 spot. By the time they won their next match on 21 September, a 45-38 win over Wimbledon, they had slipped to fourth place in the league. Also during this period, New Cross crashed out of the National Trophy, losing to West Ham 109-117 on aggregate.

With French's return and Baker back in the team, the Rangers picked up towards the end of the season, winning five out of their last six fixtures to show what might have been, but it was too late. In the end though, given the problems they had encountered from August onwards, it was a very creditable performance to finish the league in third place, equal on points with runners-up, Belle Vue.

Towards the end of the season, New Cross made history by becoming the inaugural full first-division team to undertake a tour of Sweden. Their first match was against Norrkoping Wolves, which they won 47-37, with Cyril Roger scoring a maximum. Yet again the pick of the Swedish riders was Olle Nygren who scored ten points. The second match of the tour was against a combined Swedish team, which

Alf Cole, at various times mechanic, trainer and team manger, was associated with New Cross from its opening in 1934 until 1953.

New Cross won, this time by 49 points to 35, with Cyril Roger scoring another maximum.

Cyril Roger's performances in Sweden seemed to give him extra confidence back in Britain as in his next match he scored his third consecutive full maximum, this time against Harringay.

Although the loss of Johnson and French for part of the season was a big blow it was also the case that – the Rogers and Longley apart – the other riders had not quite lived up to expectations given their successes in 1948.

Both Longley and Cyril Roger qualified for the World Championship final with Longley finishing in equal-seventh place on eight points and Roger tenth with seven.

1949 – National League Division One

8 April	H	West Ham	W	44-39
9 April	A	Belle Vue	L	23-58
11 April	A	Wimbledon	W	47-34
15 April	H	Belle Vue	W	46-38
22 April	H	Bradford	W	48-34
23 April	A	Bradford	L	34-40
29 April	H	Birmingham	W	56-28
30 April	A	Birmingham	L	38-46
6 May	H	Wembley	L	40-44
10 May	A	West Ham	L	36-48
12 May	A	Wembley	L	31-53
13 May	H	West Ham	W	54-29
20 May	H	Wimbledon	W	44-40
27 May	H	Belle Vue	W	51-33
28 May	A	Belle Vue	L	39-45
30 May	A	Wimbledon	W	50-34
3 June	H	Wembley	W	48-36
4 June	A	Bradford	L	41-42
7 June	A	West Ham	W	45-39
10 June	H	West Ham	W	55-29
17 June	H	Bradford	W	64-20
23 June	A	Wembley	L	31-53
24 June	H	Wimbledon	W	42-41
1 July	H	Birmingham	W	52-32
6 July	H	Harringay	W	63-20
8 July	A	Harringay	W	48-35
16 July	A	Belle Vue	L	40-43
26 July	A	West Ham	L	30-54
30 July	A	Bradford	L	30-54
3 August	H	Harringay	W	43-40
6 August	A	Birmingham	L	34-50
24 August	H	Belle Vue	W	46-38
29 August	A	Wimbledon	L	36-48
31 August	H	Wembley	L	38-46
9 September	A	Harringay	L	31-52
17 September	A	Birmingham	L	35-49
21 September	H	Wimbledon	W	45-38
28 September	H	Harringay	W	51-33
29 September	A	Wembley	L	32-52
5 October	H	Bradford	W	57-27

7 October	A	Harringay	W	49-34
12 October	H	Birmingham	W	50-34

P42 W24 D0 L18
For 1,817 points; Against 1,692 points
Finished 3rd (out of 8)

1949 – National Trophy

First round

Bye

Second round

17 August	H	Bristol	W	55-53
19 August	A	Bristol	W	60-47

Won 115-100 on aggregate

Semi-final

6 September	A	West Ham	L	44-64
7 September	H	West Ham	W	55-53

Lost 109-117 on aggregate

1949 – London Cup

First round

27 July	H	Wimbledon	W	57-50
1 August	A	Wimbledon	W	56-51

Won 113-101 on aggregate

Semi-final

13 September	A	West Ham	L	43-65
14 September	H	West Ham	L	38-70

Lost 81-135 on aggregate

1949 – National League Division One Averages

Rider	M	R	Pts	BP	T	CMA	FM	PM
Ron Johnson	25	94	186	17	203	8.64	2	2
Cyril Roger	42	166	308	22	330	7.95	2	4
Bill Longley	42	167	301	30	331	7.93	1	2
Eric French	36	144	230	42	272	7.56	0	2
Jeff Lloyd	42	167	275	30	305	7.31	1	0
Bert Roger	42	131	185	25	210	6.41	0	1
Bob Baker	8	17	21	5	26	6.12	0	0
Ray Moore	42	143	176	30	206	5.76	0	0
Frank Lawrence	42	115	186	29	149	5.18	0	0
Don Gray	9	19	12	5	17	3.58	0	0

1950

New Cross opened the season on 29 March with a special challenge match against 1949 league champions, Wembley. The first thing the supporters noticed was that the track surface had been changed to red shale; what they didn't notice, however, was the atmosphere in the dressing rooms. The Control Board had introduced a new smaller rear tyre for 1950, as they considered it to be safer. Some riders were very much in favour of the new tyre, but most objected to the fact that it was being made compulsory. Jeff Lloyd, as a newly elected member of the Speedway Riders' Association (SRA), held the view that there needed to be a full meeting between the Control Board and the SRA to come to some agreement. However, to keep faith with the fans who had turned up at the meeting, Lloyd, on behalf of the SRA, agreed that the meeting should go ahead on the new tyres 'under protest'. Once the meeting started, the thing the spectators noticed most about the new tyre was that it reduced the spray thrown up by a rider's back wheel and those behind were able to get closer to those in front without fear of being blinded.

The formula used for the challenge match involved using ten riders per side over 20 heats. The ten who turned out for the Rangers showed an unchanged side from that of 1949, with Johnson back alongside Longley, Lloyd, French, Moore, Lawrence, Cyril and Bert Roger, Gray and Baker.

The most obvious fact about the match was that the Wembley riders were yards faster from the gate than their New Cross counterparts, who did not seem to be able to get used to the new tyre at all. In the end, Wembley won rather easily, 70-49. Johnson won his first race, but then fell, finished fourth in his third outing and retired from the match. There was still some concern on the part of Mockford that his captain and star rider had returned too soon from his horrific injury of the year before.

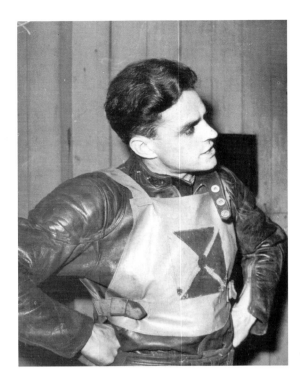

Jeff Lloyd rode for New Cross from 1947 to 1950.

A new competition, the Spring Cup, was introduced in 1950. The National League teams were split into two league groups, with the winners of each league meeting in the final. New Cross's group included Belle Vue, Bristol and Wimbledon. The formula for these matches was the same ten-rider, 20-heat formula as used in the opening challenge match.

New Cross's first match in the Spring Cup was a home tie against Belle Vue. This time, the Rangers put up a much better showing, having got used to the new tyres. French was the top man, scoring paid 14 plus one fall, but it was the reserves who did particularly well and were instrumental in winning the match for the Rangers; both Lawrence and Baker scored maximums in the 65-50 home win.

The following week, the Rangers won again, this time against Wimbledon, 65-55. Once more, the reserves were on top form, scoring 16 points out of a possible 20 between them. At the top of the order, it was French and Bert Roger who led the way. But the whole team was now beginning to gel once more, and they were able to win the next two Spring Cup matches, both away from home, the second by the colossal score of 78-42 over near neighbours Wimbledon. The whole team, with one exception, were now in their stride and scoring well. The one exception was Johnson, who seemed to tire very quickly and was having a difficult time scoring points.

Although New Cross were unbeaten in official fixtures, there was still much discontent amongst the team over the new tyre. Many other riders were also unhappy about the

An atmospheric view of the start of a race at the Frying Pan.

situation and towards the end of April, the Control Board met to consider the position and ruled that the new narrow tyre was no longer compulsory and that it was up to each rider to choose for himself which tyre he would like to ride on.

Two more Spring Cup victories followed the abandonment of the narrow tyre. The first at home was the 72-47 win over Bristol, while the second victory, at Belle Vue, was said to have been the best match seen at Belle Vue since the war. The Aces took the lead in Heat 7 and held on to it until the last heat but one when Longley and Cyril Roger's 5-1 put the Rangers in front by three points. Tension mounted inside the stadium as Belle Vue announced they would run Jack Parker and Dent Oliver in the final nominated riders' heat, while New Cross opted for Bert Roger, who at this point had scored a paid maximum, and Eric French. Belle Vue needed a 5-1 to save the match but French ensured this did not happen as he rocketed from the gate and was never in any danger. The final score was Belle Vue 58, New Cross 61, which meant that New Cross had won every one of their six Spring Cup league-phase matches.

It was, therefore, a very confident New Cross that began the National League campaign the following week at home to Bradford. Back to the normal eight-man teams, Gray and Baker were dropped, but the result was the same as the Rangers pounded the Bradford Boomerangs, 53-31. The Roger brothers and Eric French proved the backbone of their success, with Bert Roger scoring a maximum. Johnson showed a welcome return to form with paid 11 from four rides, following his partner home in every race.

The first leg of the Spring Cup final was away at West Ham's Custom House track and saw the entire Rangers' side work together as a team. There was not one weak link as they ran out victors, 73-45. With a 28-point lead from the away leg, there was little doubt as to who would win the Spring Cup. And so it proved. Even without Cyril Roger – who had crashed in his last race of the first leg and was forced to miss the return – it was once again a case of the whole team pulling together. French in particular was in scintillating form and top-scored with 17 paid 18.

Mockford decided that winning the first trophy of the 1950 season was a major cause for celebration, not just for the riders and officials but for the whole club, including the fans, so he booked the large and exclusive Pyne Brothers restaurant in Lewisham Way to hold a dinner and cabaret for the first 250 supporters to buy tickets.

With eight Spring Cup matches, including the final, and three National League matches behind them, the Rangers were still unbeaten. The next match was against their main rivals for honours, Wembley, on the latter's own track. It was a tremendous tussle but, in the end, the continued absence of Cyril Roger proved just too much for the Rangers and they lost their first official fixture of the season by the narrow margin of two points, 41-43.

Five days later on 16 May, Johnson was booked into appear in the second half at West Ham. He took an ordinary spill, which appeared at first to have no serious implications, but it was later discovered he had broken a wrist and was likely to miss several meetings. With Cyril Roger injured and now Johnson out, New Cross's promising start to the season looked as though it could soon come to an end. The next match would be another real test as it was the home league match against Wembley. Because of Johnson's absence, Cyril Roger agreed to ride but, as events proved, he was far from fit. He rode in great pain with his leg strapped up and was little more than a passenger. French, with

Bill Longley began his career at New Cross in 1938 and, apart from missing the 1946 season, remained there until 1953.

ten points, and Lawrence with eight paid nine, tried their best but the Rangers suffered their second successive defeat and their first at home as they went down 38-48.

With Johnson still out and Roger not yet recovered, a bigger defeat at Bradford, 33-51, and then another at West Ham followed and all New Cross's hopes for the season were vanishing fast. However, a recovery was just around the corner, as Cyril Roger's problems eased and he was able to get back to match-winning form with an 11-point score to back up French's maximum in a convincing 55-29 home victory over Wimbledon. This was the first of a run of four-straight victories, including one away at Bristol. Throughout these four matches, French in particular was in devastating form. In fact he was riding so well during this period that he was chosen as the next British Match Race Championship challenger for Jack Parker. But the team wasn't just relying on him as he was receiving strong backing from the Roger brothers and Longley, who, since being appointed acting captain in place of Johnson, was now riding as well as ever. Lawrence was also proving to be a great asset as replacement for Johnson. Lloyd was the only member of the team who seemed to be struggling a bit, while Moore and Baker at reserve were doing all that could be asked of them.

The run came to an end at Birmingham on 17 June, due to the fact that Longley had been injured in the second half of New Cross's match against Belle Vue, suffering a cracked rib. But even then, it was only by a two-point margin and a last-heat defeat as the Rangers lost 43-41.

The first leg of French's British Match Race Championship challenge against Jack Parker took place at New Cross. French said he was hoping for rain as he reckoned his chances would be better on a wet track. Precisely two minutes before the scheduled start of the meeting, the heavens opened and within just a few minutes the track was completely waterlogged. The rain stopped almost as suddenly as it had started and the New Cross track staff set to work with buckets and brooms clearing the water away,

Bert Roger and Eric French lead West Ham's Kid Curtis.

while the stadium's trailer pump was also brought into use. Forty-five minutes later, the ACU Steward declared the track fit to ride and French, rubbing his hands with glee, did exactly what he had said he would do if the track was wet and completely outrode Parker, winning the first leg 2-0. Parker had won the title in 1947 and had so far swept aside all ten challenges from the world's top riders. Only two of those challengers had even won a leg, yet here was French one-up.

The second leg of the Match Race Championship took place on Parker's home track, Belle Vue, on 1 July. Naturally, Parker was the red-hot favourite to win on his own track but as the tapes went up for the first race, French shot into the lead. By the end of the second lap, he had built up a lead of two lengths. As they came round the last bend of the last lap, French took up a position in the centre of the track. Parker went out wide behind him and then cut in, shooting through on the inside to just pip French on the line. It was the nearest French was to come to lifting the title, as Parker won the second race more easily and then won the decider at Birmingham, 2-0. Nevertheless, it had been the most difficult challenge Parker had faced and when French continued his brilliant mid-season run – scoring eight paid 12 for England in the second Test match at Belle Vue – it only served to confirm French's position as one of the best riders in the country. The London Riders' Championship was another triumph for New Cross riders as Cyril Roger took the title with a 15-point maximum, followed closely by his brother, Bert, on 14.

On 5 July, the team were all back together again as both Johnson and Longley took their places in the line-up. They celebrated with a convincing 59-25 victory over Bradford, with French scoring a paid maximum and Longley, showing that his absence had not affected him, adding paid 11 from four rides.

At this stage of the season, New Cross were lying in second place in the league behind Wembley, so the next match at the Empire Stadium was a vital one for both teams. As befitted the occasion, it proved to be an extremely close and exciting match and after nine heats the scores were level at 27-all. The riders lining up for Heat 10 were Longley and Bert Roger for New Cross and George Wilks and reserve Alf Bottoms for Wembley. Longley fell and Bottoms made a headlong dive into the safety fence after hitting Longley's machine. He was taken to hospital with a badly damaged knee. With Bottoms unable to take part and Longley excluded, only two riders lined up for the rerun. The race developed into a classic match race and Roger, who was just behind, suddenly sped past the Wembley rider on the final straight to cross the line in first place. But the steward excluded him for unfair riding and the heat was therefore won 3-0 by Wembley. Everyone in the stadium, apart from the steward, seemed to be at a complete loss as to why Roger had been excluded. In the pits, the New Cross riders were incensed and decided to walk out of the meeting. They were actually on their way to the dressing room when Mockford came down and ordered them to complete the meeting. He said he would bang in an official protest to the Control Board. However, the incident upset the team and they lost heart, finally going down 36-45. Strangely enough, after this incident, it was announced that Bert Roger would be Parker's next challenger for the Match Race title. He celebrated this announcement by scoring 14 points in the third Test match in which no less than five New Cross riders had been chosen to represent their respective countries, French and the Roger brothers for England and Johnson and Longley for Australia.

Although he was now riding better than previously in the season, Lloyd thought that a move away from the Frying Pan would help him and consequently put in a transfer request. This was granted by Mockford and Smith, who felt it was bad for speedway for just one or two teams to be so strong that they dominated the league every year. Their view was that as New Cross was one of these teams, it would be good for speedway if they reduced their strength, so they were happy to let Lloyd move to one of the weaker teams and off he went to Harringay. His place in the team was taken by Lawrence, while Gray was reinstated at reserve to take Lawrence's place.

Although Lloyd had not enjoyed the best of seasons in 1950, his departure upset the balance of the team and the team went through a bad patch, losing both legs to Wimbledon in the first round of the London Cup and both legs of the first-round National Trophy tie against Belle Vue. As well as Lloyd's transfer, there were other reasons for these losses: Cyril Roger missed three of the ties due to a stomach complaint, Johnson was still not back to full fitness and Longley also began to struggle. From having six top-class riders, New Cross were now being carried mainly by French and Bert Roger. And

Ray Moore rode for New Cross from 1946 to 1951, but never lived up to his early promise. He tried a comeback in 1960, riding in just one meeting.

then, just as things couldn't seem to get any worse, Johnson was knocked unconscious after falling in Heat 5 of the league match against Harringay. At first, the injuries did not seem to be too bad, but, as it turned out, it meant the end of the season for him.

Even when Cyril Roger was able to return a fortnight later, New Cross's woes were not ended as Lawrence then sustained an injury that put him out for a couple of matches. His place was taken by a young junior, and former cycle-speedway star, Ronnie Genz.

When Lawrence returned, on 18 August, the team, apart from Johnson, managed to remain at full strength for six matches, during which time they had three good home wins, including a 62-22 victory over Bristol in which both Rogers and French scored paid maximums, and three away losses. Although these three were generally performing well – both home and away – the rest of the team seemed to have forgotten how to ride away from the Old Kent Road circuit. Longley, in particular, was most disappointing, scoring a total of just three points in the three matches.

New Cross had, by now, lost all hope of winning the league title and even the chance of the runner-up spot disappeared when Bert Roger became the latest injury victim and missed the last four matches of the league season, all of which New Cross lost.

Film star Trevor Howard (centre) presents Cyril Roger (right) with the 1950 London Riders' Championship trophy. Cyril's brother, Bert (left), was runner-up.

The season, which had started with so much promise, had been wrecked by injury and Mockford and Smith may well have regretted letting Lloyd go. Johnson, slowly returning to form after his horrific injury the season before, suffered two further injuries and only managed nine league matches. Longley missed several meetings and, when he did come back, was not the rider he had been. Lawrence, performing well as a second string, even to the extent of scoring three paid maximums, was forced to miss a number of meetings and the Roger brothers also lost out on seven matches between them. Only two riders were ever-presents, French and Moore.

French's gradual year-on-year improvement continued and at one time there is no doubt he was right up there with best, as his match race series with Jack Parker showed, but towards the end of the season, even he began to lose form. Along with French, it was the Roger brothers who kept New Cross's hopes alive for as long as they could. As well as their consistent points scoring, individually both brothers did well. Bert was chosen as challenger for the British Match Race Championship, although he lost both legs to Parker, while Cyril won the London Riders' Championship. Sadly, his injury problems interfered with his chances of qualifying for the World Championship final, but he did manage to make it as reserve. On the night he showed what might have been as he scored five points from two rides, beating, amongst others, Vic Duggan and Jack Young.

In French, Lawrence and the Roger brothers, New Cross had four riders who could still improve and if Johnson and Longley could get back to their best form, there was still hope that the Rangers would be fighting it out for honours in 1951 – but they were very big ifs.

1950 – National League Division One

26 April	H	Bradford	W	53–31
3 May	H	Harringay	W	51–33
5 May	A	Harringay	W	47–37
11 May	A	Wembley	L	41–43
17 May	H	Wembley	L	36–48
24 May	H	Birmingham	W	60–24
27 May	A	Bradford	L	33–51
30 May	A	West Ham	L	39–45
31 May	H	Wimbledon	W	55–29
7 June	H	West Ham	W	54–29
9 June	A	Bristol	W	43–41
14 June	H	Belle Vue	W	59–29
17 June	A	Birmingham	L	41–43
21 June	H	Bristol	W	64–20
1 July	A	Belle Vue	W	44–40
5 July	H	Bradford	W	59–25
14 July	A	Harringay	L	35–49
2 August	H	Harringay	W	47–35
16 August	H	West Ham	W	50–34
18 August	A	Bristol	L	36–48
30 August	H	Belle Vue	W	54–30
2 September	A	Bradford	L	27–57
6 September	H	Birmingham	W	47–37
9 September	A	Belle Vue	L	23–61
13 September	H	Bristol	W	62–22
18 September	A	Wimbledon	L	23–61
26 September	A	West Ham	L	29–55
27 September	H	Wembley	L	39–45
4 October	H	Wimbledon	L	38–48
7 October	A	Birmingham	L	34–49

P32 W16 D1 L15

For 1,401 points; Against 1,280 points

Finished 4th (out of 9)

1950 – National Trophy

First round

26 July	H	Belle Vue	L	48-60
29 July	A	Belle Vue	L	28-80

Lost 76-140 on aggregate

1950 – London Cup

19 July	H	Wimbledon	L	45-62
24 July	A	Wimbledon	L	33-74

Lost 78-136 on aggregate

1950 – Spring Cup

League phase

5 April	H	Belle Vue	W	65-50
12 April	H	Wimbledon	W	65-55
15 April	A	Bristol	W	61-59
17 April	A	Wimbledon	W	78-42
19 April	H	Bristol	W	72-47
22 April	A	Belle Vue	W	61-58

P6 W6 D0 L0

For 402 points; Against 311 points

Finished 1st (out of 4)

Final

9 May	A	West Ham	W	73-45
10 May	H	West Ham	W	70-50

Won Spring Cup 143-95 on aggregate

New Cross Spring Cup champions

1950 – National League Division One Averages

Rider	M	R	Pts	BP	T	CMA	FM	PM
Cyril Roger	29	116	260	7	267	9.21	3	1
Bert Roger	28	112	236	17	253	9.04	4	3
Eric French	32	128	267	15	282	8.81	2	4
Jeff Lloyd	18	72	105	24	129	7.17	0	1
Bill Longley	29	115	175	28	203	7.06	2	1
Frank Lawrence	30	113	137	28	165	5.84	0	3
Ray Moore	32	97	106	12	123	5.07	0	1
Ron Johnson	9	27	29	5	34	5.04	0	0
Don Gray	16	38	27	8	35	3.68	0	0
Bob Baker	26	67	58	7	65	3.88	0	0
Ronnie Genz	6	11	1	1	2	0.73	0	0

1951

The 'ifs' were enough for Mockford and Smith to put in a request to the Control Board to allow them to sign up young Swedish star Olle Nygren, who had so impressed them in the last couple of seasons. The Control Board turned down their request as they felt that the Rangers were still strong on paper, and instead allocated Nygren to Harringay.

Over the winter, New Cross experimented with a new type of starting surface. At the beginning of 1950, the concrete starting area had been introduced to try and make starts fairer, but, during the season, a number of weaknesses had been revealed. This was particularly true in bad weather, where starting was particularly treacherous on a concrete surface and riders often snaked away from the start, sliding all over the place. To overcome this, New Cross experimented with a new substance known as flexine, which was a substance made up of concrete, granite and synthetic rubber. Tests were carried out in January by Moore and Longley watched by representatives from other tracks. The experiment was not a success, however, and it was decided to revert to a tarmac starting area.

Early in 1951, Cecil Smith announced he was giving up his interest in New Cross speedway after twenty-three years' involvement as Fred Mockford's partner at Crystal Palace and the Frying Pan. Mockford put out a press statement saying:

Cecil's decision was sudden. He got in touch with me, with the result that I have bought the whole of his shares and I am now the 100 per cent proprietor of London Motor Sports Ltd, the company which stages speedway at New Cross… For a year or so now his other interests have meant that control of speedway matters at New Cross have fallen more on my shoulders so that the change will not be so violent as the uninitiated may think.

Although Nygren was ruled out of the New Cross starting squad, two other Swedes, Sune Karlsson and Lennart Carlstrom, attended the New Cross pre-season practice session. Johnson had still not been declared fit enough to ride and the captain's job was handed over to Eric French, with Longley as vice-captain.

The Rangers' first match of the season was an away challenge match at Bristol, with the New Cross team consisting of French, Longley, the Roger brothers, Lawrence, Moore, Baker and Gray. It was not a promising start as they lost 37-47. Following this match, Bob Baker was transferred to Yarmouth with Eric Minall taking his place as reserve.

Shortly after this, Mockford wrote in the New Cross programme: 'I do not think our line-up is weak, but it does not provide a safety margin. If injuries come our way then we shall be up against it.' Sadly, this was to prove very prophetic.

The first league match was not until 7 May and before then New Cross took part in a series of challenge matches. Taking these matches as an early guide, it looked as though New Cross would be struggling to maintain even fourth place in the league. Losses away were the norm and victories hard to come by at home. Sure enough, when the league matches started, New Cross found themselves on the wrong end of a 51-33 scoreline away at Wimbledon and then could only draw 42-42 with the same team at home. The Roger brothers, French and Lawrence were all riding reasonably well, but there was a long tail behind them. Longley was having difficulty recapturing the form everyone knew he was capable of, Moore had odd flashes but was not the rider he had been two seasons ago and Gray and Minall were not really up to the required standard.

Minall was dropped after three matches and Genz brought back into the team. Two good performances, home and away, against Bristol, gave some hope. The first was a 46-38 away win, the second a 48-34 home win. Even so, the team was still being carried mainly by the 'Big Four'. After this double over Bristol, the pattern of away losses and narrow home wins reasserted itself, until the Rangers pulled off another double, this time over the hapless Bradford, who were by far and away the weakest team in the league. In the meantime, Genz had broken his shoulder in a crash at West Ham and was replaced by Bob Aldridge.

The match against Birmingham on 13 June proved to be a thrilling encounter with the Rangers just coming out on top, 43-41, but it was Heat 2 of the match that was to put paid to New Cross's season. The race was twice rerun. Only one Birmingham rider rode in the second rerun, as Lionel Watling had been excluded, but on the second lap, Bert Roger fell and Longley laid down his machine to avoid hitting him. With three points at stake, both riders picked themselves up and completed the race. Bert Roger came out again in Heat 10 to beat Birmingham's star rider, Alan Hunt. But what was not known at the time was that Roger had, in fact, fractured his wrist in that Heat 2 fall. It was to be the last time Roger rode for New Cross for eight matches and in those eight matches, the Rangers did not manage a single win.

In the middle of this doom and gloom, the Rangers welcomed back a familiar face as, Ron Johnson returned on 20 June, to take his place in the side. But it was no fairytale comeback for the fans' hero, as he worked hard but unsuccessfully to regain his old form.

With things getting desperate, Mockford looked around for a rider to strengthen the team. Three riders came to his attention: the first was a young Swedish rider, Rune Sormander, the second an Australian, Merv Harding – known as the Red Devil because he wore red leathers – and the third, the former Southampton star Tom Oakley. In the end, it was Oakley who found himself in the orange and black of New Cross as he made his debut on 14 July at Bradford, scoring six points. With his arrival, Moore was transferred to Fleetwood for £300.

Bert Roger returned on 25 July to face Belle Vue at home, but it made no difference, as the Rangers lost their ninth match on the trot. Two more defeats followed, this time in the semi-final of the London Cup to Wembley, as the Rangers were defeated 63–45 at home and then 70–33 away. Following these two defeats, Johnson was loaned out to Glasgow in a bid to give his confidence a boost by racing at a lower level. In his place, Mockford signed up Harold McNaughton from Ipswich.

After a twelfth successive defeat, this time in the league at home to Harringay, Mockford made public some correspondence he'd had with the SRA earlier in the season when he was attempting to sign up Rune Sormander. The correspondence centred on the SRA's refusal to support the signing of more foreign riders to British speedway teams. Mockford wanted to know why this was the case, as he felt that weak teams like his own had nowhere else to turn to and also that foreign stars would improve the standard of racing. The SRA pointed out that it was the Control Board's decision whether to allow the signing of Sormander and that they only had one vote on the board. They felt, therefore, that Mockford should take the matter up with the Control Board and not them. Mockford's feeling however was that if the SRA had supported the application then so would the Control Board.

New Cross's disastrous run finally came to an end on 22 August when, for the first time in 14 matches, the Rangers tasted victory as they defeated Bristol 51–33 at home. They followed this up the following week with a 65–43 win over West Ham in the first leg of the National Trophy second round. After the match, Mockford said: 'I'm exceedingly pleased with the way the boys have ridden this evening. I think the 22-point lead will be enough to see us through on aggregate.' And he was right as 'the boys' managed to restrict West Ham to a 16-point lead back at Custom House, thereby going through 111–105 on aggregate. It was the first minor success all season but, unfortunately, it was followed by a further five consecutive defeats in the league and two more in the National Trophy semi-final, the second of these by the massive score of 29–78, as they went down and out to Wembley, 82–133 on aggregate.

There was a short final flourish to the season as New Cross won two out of their last three matches, but it was a season the manager, the riders and the supporters couldn't wait to see the back of. In the end, they just avoided last place in the league thanks to victory over Bradford in the very last match of the season. They finished with just nine wins to their name out of 32 matches.

Bert Roger's mid-season injury had not helped, but all the riders, with the sole exception of Lawrence, were down on their previous year's performances. Longley, in particular, had a disastrous season with his average dropping from 7.06 to 4.90 and, of course, Johnson's much hoped-for comeback to the big time never materialised. Not one of the team made it to the World Championship final – the first time New Cross had not been represented on the big night since the World Championship started in 1936.

Because of the team's poor performance and because of other external matters, such as the increase in entertainment tax and the growing number of people with televisions, the New Cross attendance figures fell dramatically during 1951.

1951 – National League Division One

7 May	A	Wimbledon	L	33-51
9 May	H	Wimbledon	D	42-42
11 Ma	A	Bristol	W	46-38
16 May	H	Bristol	W	48-34
23 May	H	Harringay	W	45-39
25 May	A	Harringay	L	34-50
30 May	H	West Ham	W	43-41
2 June	A	Bradford	L	40-44
6 June	H	Bradford	W	56-28
13 June	H	Birmingham	W	43-41
15 June	A	Harringay	L	38-45
18 June	A	Wimbledon	L	35-49
20 June	H	Belle Vue	L	39-45
23 June	A	Belle Vue	L	31-52
4 July	H	Wembley	L	29-53
6 July	A	Bristol	L	28-56
14 July	A	Bradford	L	39-45
18 July	H	Wimbledon	L	39-45
25 July	H	Belle Vue	L	39-45
8 August	H	Harringay	L	35-47
12 August	H	Bristol	W	51-33
21 August	A	West Ham	L	40-44
25 August	A	Birmingham	L	33-51
30 August	A	Wembley	L	28-55
5 September	H	Birmingham	L	38-46
8 September	A	Belle Vue	L	36-48
12 September	H	Wembley	L	35-49
22 September	A	Birmingham	L	25-59

3 October	H	West Ham	W	49–34
10 October	H	Bradford	W	54–29
18 October	A	Wembley	L	27–57

P32 W9 D1 L22

For 1,234 points; Against 1,443 points

Finished 8th (out of 9)

1951 – National Trophy

First round

Bye

Second Round

| 29 August | H | West Ham | W | 65–43 |
| 4 September | A | West Ham | L | 46–62 |

Won 111–105 on aggregate

Semi-final

| 26 September | H | Wembley | L | 53–55 |
| 4 October | A | Wembley | L | 29–78 |

Lost 82–133 on aggregate

1951 – London Cup

First round

Bye

Semi-final

| 1 August | H | Wembley | L | 45–63 |
| 2 August | A | Wembley | L | 38–70 |

Lost 83–133 on aggregate

1951 – National League Division One Averages

Rider	M	R	Pts	BP	T	CMA	FM	PM
Cyril Roger	31	122	264	5	269	8.82	4	0
Eric French	32	125	253	9	262	8.38	1	0
Bert Roger	21	82	162	3	165	8.05	3	0
Frank Lawrence	31	124	174	26	200	6.45	0	1
Tom Oakley	15	60	81	13	94	6.27	0	0
Bill Longley	31	120	125	22	147	4.90	0	0
Ron Johnson	7	17	13	3	16	3.76	0	0
Don Gray	32	103	81	15	96	3.73	0	0
Harold McNaughton	9	21	16	3	19	3.62	0	0
Ray Moore	19	67	48	12	60	3.58	0	0
Ronnie Genz	10	21	9	3	12	2.29	0	0
Bob Aldridge	8	16	4	2	6	1.50	0	0

1952

Just before the season started at the beginning of April, the New Cross retained list was announced as Eric French, Bert Roger, Cyril Roger, Bob Roger, Frank Lawrence, Tom Oakley, Bill Longley, Ronnie Genz, Olle Nygren, Merv Harding, Ron Johnson and Ray Moore. Bob Roger, the youngest of the Roger brothers, had been transferred over the winter from Exeter. Moore had returned from Fleetwood, following the latter's demise at the end of the 1951 season. Although placed on their retained list, the position of both Harding and Nygren was still unclear as the Control Board had not yet sanctioned the transfer of either. Harding's move from second division Glasgow was eventually approved, but the position with Nygren became very complicated. General approval to his inclusion in the New Cross side was given on condition that he was available to ride in all of New Cross's official fixtures and a labour permit applied for. However, Nygren's team in Sweden, the Norrkoping Wolves, said they would only allow him to sign for New Cross on the understanding that he would need to return to Sweden from time to time to help them out and, therefore, would probably need to miss four or five meetings in England. The Control Board would not agree to this.

With the situation regarding Nygren still unresolved, Mockford hit on the novel idea of sending Bob Roger to Sweden in Nygren's place so that he would not need to be recalled during the season, but, although both New Cross and Norrkoping were happy with this arrangement, the Control Board would not sanction it as they felt Roger was not the equal of Nygren. In the end, discussions between New Cross, Norrkoping and the Control Board broke down and Mockford was forced to give up on signing Nygren for the second year running.

On 12 April, the SS *Otranto* set sail from Southampton to Australia. On board was Ron Johnson, who had decided to retire from the sport and return home. Although

Johnson was no longer in the team and was no longer the rider he had been when at the top of his powers, it was nevertheless a very emotional moment for everyone associated with New Cross, from Mockford right down to the fan on the terrace. In his time with the club he had won many honours including the British Individual Match Race Championship and the London Riders' Championship twice. He had finished runner-up in both the old Star Riders' Championship and the post-war Riders' Championship and had been chosen to ride for Australia on 55 occasions, scoring a total of 351 points. As he boarded the ship he said: 'I've enjoyed myself as a speedway rider. I gave everything I had and I am very grateful to all the supporters who gave me encouragement.'

New Cross put up a very poor performance in their opening league fixture, away at Belle Vue, as they went down 31-53. By way of a complete contrast, the first home meeting resulted in a magnificent 56-28 win over Bradford. Over the next few matches the pattern of big away losses and big home wins became something of the norm, apart from a good 46-36 victory away from home at league newcomers Norwich, on 26 April. For the first seven matches, New Cross were able to put out the same eight riders, the three Rogers, French, Lawrence, Oakley, Harding and Longley. This early-season form showed that once again the main scoring was coming from Cyril and Bert Roger, and French, along with Harding, who was contributing a regular seven or eight points each match. The first change in the line-up came on 2 May when Longley missed the match at Bristol. He had been struggling in the reserve berth and had put in a transfer request. Mockford agreed and placed a £500 price tag on him and dropped him from the team. His place was taken by Genz. As it turned out, his inclusion proved to be a masterstroke as he scored eight paid nine from three rides at reserve, helping the Rangers to their second away win of the season, 49-35.

With two away wins now under their belt, New Cross found themselves at the top of the National League, although they had raced more matches than any other team. They had ten points from eight matches, while West Ham, in second place had eight from only five. Just as it looked as if New Cross were recovering from their disastrous 1951 season they were struck by another blow as Cyril Roger suffered a recurrence of his stomach complaint and was sidelined for nine matches. He had scored no points in the win over Bristol, saying: 'Every ride seems like a nightmare these days… not much point going on like that.'

With Roger's absence, Longley returned to the team and put up his best performance of the season, top-scoring with eight points at Birmingham, but it was a poor New Cross performance as they went down 50-34.

The Rangers' next match was at home to Wembley. With two heats to go the score was New Cross 39, Wembley 32. A win for the home side looked a certainty, but there then followed two of the most controversial heats ever seen at the Frying Pan. In Heat 13 Bob Roger and Wembley's Eric Williams were fighting it out for first place. Coming into the last bend on the third lap, Williams took Roger wide and almost into the fence forcing him to slow up. Williams's teammate, George Wilks, was able to nip through on the inside giving Wembley a 5-1. The New Cross manager, Alf Cole, immediately phoned the steward, Alan Day, to protest and call for Williams to be excluded for unfair riding. Day replied that it was a borderline case and he was going to allow the result to stand. Although still not happy with the decision, New Cross were not unduly worried as the score was still fairly comfortably in their favour at New Cross 40, Wembley 37, and with the unbeaten Bert Roger out in the last heat they felt confident enough. As the last heat started the crowd's jeers at the steward's decision turned to cheers as Roger led from the gate, giving the Rangers the three points they needed to be sure of victory, but as Roger entered the first bend on the third lap he overslid and a big groan went up from the crowd. Coming up fast behind, Genz hit Roger's machine and went down. There were now two fallen riders and their machines on the track along with four ambulancemen and some rakers who had rushed out to provide assistance. Everybody in the stadium expected the red lights to go on, but they didn't and the two Wembley riders coasted home for five unopposed points, making the final score New Cross 40, Wembley 42. As far as the crowd was concerned this was the second time in two heats that the steward had made a dreadful decision in Wembley's favour and they were absolutely incensed. The announcer was unable to make any announcements for several minutes due to the noise, so, in the end, Mockford himself came on to the public address to say that he would be sending a letter to the Control Board immediately protesting about the steward's handling of the meeting. After the meeting, a number of fans stormed Mockford's office demanding further action be taken against Mr Day, though, eventually, they left peacefully enough. Mockford commented, 'It was a regrettable end to a grand match.'

This home defeat was a big blow to any lingering hopes New Cross might have retained of taking the league title. The next five matches went the way of the early-season ones, with three away losses and two home wins. In Cyril's absence, Bert Roger had now taken over as top man and in all five matches was the Rangers' top scorer. He received consistently good support from his captain, Eric French, but the rest of the team's form was patchy. Lawrence was just about holding his own, but Oakley's form had gone downhill dramatically and Harding was proving to be inconsistent. After his eight points against Birmingham, Longley was back amongst the twos and threes, along with the third Roger brother, Bob.

As if things weren't bad enough, Cyril Roger chose this moment to bang in a transfer request on his doctor's advice, saying he wished to ride for a less-fashionable, provincial team as he thought this would be better for his health. Mockford agreed reluctantly, placing a fee of £2,700 on his star rider's head, but said he would rather have a rider in exchange.

New Cross's next matches were the first-round legs of the London Cup, in which they had been drawn against West Ham. The Hammers had a very similar record to the Rangers, with wins at home and generally poor results away, so it looked as though it was going to be a matter of which team would do least badly away. The first leg was at Custom House with West Ham taking the tie, 63-45. Given the fortunes of the two teams this season there was still all to play for for New Cross and a 16,000 crowd turned out to see a tremendous return. The Hammers' 18-point advantage was whittled down to just four by the interval, but West Ham hung on, winning the tie 112–103 on aggregate. The real difference between the two teams was the performance of their star riders. While West Ham's Jack Young completed an 18-point maximum, Bert Roger failed to win a single race. The Rangers' next home match, against Wimbledon, provided a nail-biting finish. The lead had changed hands no fewer than seven times during the match but going into the last heat the scores were New Cross 40, Wimbledon 37. Needing just a second-place finish to be sure of victory, the Rangers pair was Lawrence and Genz, while Wimbledon tracked

A spectacular action shot showing Bert Roger rounding Birmingham's Wilbur Lamoreaux at New Cross.

American star Ernie Roccio and the young up-and-coming Cyril Maidment. It was Roccio who got away from the start followed by Lawrence. Lawrence held the vital second place for just over two laps, but then Maidment powered his way past not only Lawrence but his own partner as well to give the Dons a 5-1 and a narrow 42-41 victory.

With the news that Cyril Roger was to return to the New Cross line-up after all, Mockford took the opportunity to transfer Oakley to Bristol for £300. Oakley had been a big disappointment and had been unable to get going all year. Oakley himself hoped that a move away from a big London club would boost his confidence.

Cyril Roger's return to the New Cross track took place on 18 June in the London Riders' Championship. As expected he was very rusty and only managed five points. His brother, Bert, finished equal-second with 12 points behind Wimbledon's young up-and-coming star Ronnie Moore, who completely dominated the meeting with a flawless maximum.

Steward Alan Day was in trouble with the New Cross crowd again in their next meeting against Belle Vue. In Heat 6, the Aces' Ken Sharples tangled with Cyril Roger who fell as a result. Mr Day put on the red lights and excluded Sharples. When Roger went back out on to the track for the rerun he was told that he was not permitted to ride. After five minutes of frantic telephone calls and consultations around the track and in the pits, the steward refused to change his decision and Cyril's place was taken by his brother Bob. Once again the crowd were outraged at this seemingly perverse decision given by Mr Day. No one apart, presumably, from Mr Day himself, could understand why he had prevented Roger from riding. All the crowd knew was that it was yet another bad decision made against the interests of the Rangers. In this case, however, it didn't matter too much as New Cross won the match 48-35.

With Cyril Roger now returned and working his way back to fitness, the team was back to full strength. But not for long! Just a week or so later, Harding broke his forearm in a bad crash at Liverpool in the first heat of a World Championship qualifying round. With Harding out, Mockford once again turned his attentions to Sweden in the hope of finding a replacement. Because of the injury to Harding, both the SRA and the Control Board were more sympathetic to his request this time and agreed to New Cross signing a Swedish rider on loan. Mockford's first target was Bo Andersson, but he too was injured – suffering from a broken ankle collected in a World Championship qualifying round – so, in the end, it was the twenty-eight-year-old Sune Karlsson who came to England to wear the Maltese Cross.

Karlsson's debut came in New Cross's second-round National Trophy tie at home against Poole. Although Poole was only a second division side they had already knocked out first division Norwich, so they were not a team to be taken lightly, but the Rangers, now up to full strength again, gave them a good mauling as they thrashed them 75-33. Even better for the Rangers was the fact that Karlsson scored a paid six-ride maximum.

Between them, Ron Johnson (left) and Fred Mockford spent over sixty years at New Cross.

With a 42-point lead over their second division rivals, New Cross must have felt that their place in the semi-final was already booked, but they received the fright of their lives as Poole fought back on their own track to such an extent that they just needed a 4-2 in the last heat to force a draw and a 5-1 to go through. Unfortunately for them, but very fortunately for New Cross, Terry Small fell on the first bend and the Rangers just squeaked through, losing 72-36 on the night but winning 111-105 on aggregate.

The next away match, against first division opposition in the league, actually proved much easier for New Cross as Cyril Roger's continuing improvement and Karlsson once again helped the Rangers to a 45-39 win over home specialists West Ham. The return fixture at New Cross the following night saw Cyril Roger back to his absolute best as he scored 11 points, including a magnificent win over the World Champion, Jack Young. Behind for two laps, the home man rode a perfect first corner on the third lap and flashed through to beat his man. As he crossed the winning line, he received a terrific ovation. Once again with excellent support from Karlsson, who registered three heat wins, the Rangers scored a convincing 49-35 victory.

To show he was still a force to be reckoned with, Bert Roger scored two full maximums in the next two matches, one away to Bradford and the second at home to Bristol, both of which New Cross won. After all their mid-season problems, New Cross were now back in business. In Cyril and Bert Roger and Karlsson, they had three of the best heat leaders in the league and with effective support from French and Lawrence, they had five riders who could hold their own with any team. Their real problem was their tail, as Longley, Bob Roger and Genz tried hard but were just not getting amongst the points. Still, it was a far cry from the previous season and even from earlier in the present season.

Next up for New Cross was the home leg of the National Trophy semi-final against Harringay. In spite of their recent form it proved to be a dismal evening for the Rangers and, strangely enough, it was Bill Longley who fought a lone battle against the Racers, scoring 12 points. In fact, the Rangers put up a much better display in the second leg, with French scoring an 18-point maximum, but it wasn't enough to get them through to the final and they went out 121-94 on aggregate.

Two more away league defeats followed, but both French and Karlsson were complaining about not feeling well. Karlsson was, in fact, found to have been riding with two broken ribs. His comment when told was: 'I must find a hospital some time.' With five matches left in the season, Karlsson returned to Sweden to have his ribs seen to and French went with him for a rest. It was hoped both would be back within two weeks.

With the departure of French and Karlsson for a while, Harding attempted a comeback to help out his team and rode with his arm still in plaster in what turned out to be a disastrous meeting for New Cross. Not only did they lose 53-31 at home to Harringay, but Bert Roger broke his collarbone in a fall in the second half and was ruled out for the rest of the season. Although by this time New Cross had nothing really to fight for in the league – a spot in mid-table now being more or less assured – it was a personal tragedy for Bert Roger; he had qualified for the World Championship final for the first time and now found himself unable to take part.

French returned in time for the last four fixtures and rode better than he had done all season, turning in two full maximums in the last three matches, Karlsson never did return and Harding rode in just one more match before deciding he was not really fit enough to come back. With a much depleted team, New Cross even lost their last home match to bottom of the table Norwich. In the end, the Rangers finished seventh out of ten.

New Cross had started the season with a strong team but they suffered more than most through injury and illness. On an individual level, both Bert and Cyril Roger qualified for the World Championship final, although Bert was unable to take his place. Cyril had a poor night, scoring just two points and finishing in fifteenth position.

The only real honours that came New Cross's way during 1952 was Bert Roger being appointed captain of the England Test team and Sune Karlsson winning the Swedish Championship.

1952 – National League Division One

12 April	A	Belle Vue	L	31–53
16 April	H	Bradford	W	56–28
18 April	A	Harringay	L	34–50
23 April	H	Wimbledon	W	58–26
26 April	A	Norwich	W	46–36
29 April	A	West Ham	L	40–43
30 April	H	Norwich	W	56–28
2 May	A	Bristol	W	49–35
7 May	H	Harringay	L	41–42
10 May	A	Birmingham	L	34–50
14 May	H	Wembley	L	40–42
21 May	H	West Ham	W	48–36
24 May	A	Belle Vue	L	35–48
28 May	H	Birmingham	W	45–39
29 May	A	Wembley	L	33–51
31 May	A	Bradford	L	29–55
11 June	H	Wimbledon	L	41–42
20 June	A	Bristol	L	37–47
25 June	H	Belle Vue	W	48–35
28 June	A	Norwich	D	42–42
2 July	H	Bristol	W	45–39
9 July	H	Birmingham	L	30–53
11 July	A	Harringay	L	32–52
16 July	H	Wembley	L	41–43
29 July	A	West Ham	W	45–39
30 July	H	West Ham	W	49–35
2 August	A	Bradford	W	50–34
6 August	H	Bristol	W	47–37
28 August	A	Wembley	L	39–45
1 September	A	Wimbledon	L	35–49
3 September	H	Bradford	W	44–40
10 September	H	Harringay	L	31–53
22 September	A	Wimbledon	L	34–50
24 September	H	Belle Vue	W	45–39
27 September	A	Birmingham	L	35–49
1 October	H	Norwich	L	35–48

P36 W15 D1 L20

For 1,480 points; Against 1,533 points

Finished 7th (out of 10)

1952 – National Trophy

First round

Bye

Second round

| 23 July | H | Poole | W | 75–33 |
| 26 July | A | Poole | L | 36–72 |

Won 111–105 on aggregate

Semi-final

| 13 August | H | Harringay | L | 43–64 |
| 15 August | A | Harringay | L | 51–57 |

Lost 94–121 on aggregate

1952 – London Cup

First round

| 3 June | A | West Ham | L | 45–63 |
| 4 June | H | West Ham | W | 58–49 |

Lost 103–112 on aggregate

1952 – National League Division One Averages

Rider	M	R	Pts	BP	T	CMA	FM	PM
Bert Roger	32	125	268	10	278	8.90	5	0
Eric French	35	139	275	24	299	8.60	5	1
Sune Karlsson	8	31	55	5	60	7.74	0	0
Cyril Roger	27	106	197	6	203	7.66	0	0
Merv Harding	23	92	150	18	168	7.30	0	0
Frank Lawrence	36	139	172	26	198	5.70	0	1
Bill Longley	35	118	131	24	155	5.25	0	0
Bob Roger	36	99	95	17	112	4.53	0	0
Tom Oakley	17	65	63	10	73	4.49	0	0
Ronnie Genz	29	81	69	14	83	4.10	0	0

1953

Over the close season, Mockford once again tried to sign up Olle Nygren and was once again turned down by the Control Board. Mockford pointed out in vain that Karlsson would not be returning and that it would therefore be a very weak New Cross who would take their place in the National League.

Apart from Karlsson, the line-up was the same as in 1952, the three Roger brothers, French, Lawrence, Longley, Harding and Genz. Just as the season was about to start, however, Harding told Mockford that he was still not fit enough and would probably miss at least the first month. With this news, Mockford returned to the Control Board, who finally relented and allowed New Cross to sign up Nygren for one month, pending Harding's return. Mockford immediately issued a statement saying: 'New Cross will give serious thoughts to discontinuing speedway if Nygren's permit is not renewed.'

For the time being however, Mockford had got his man and the Rangers opened the season taking part in a new competition, which had been specially created for Coronation Year, the Coronation Cup. This was run on league lines and consisted of all the National League Division One teams.

The opening fixture was away at Belle Vue, but it was not a good start as the Rangers lost 34-50. However, they made a much better showing in the first home match as they beat Harringay, 56-28, with French, Nygren, and the three Roger brothers all riding well. A new name came into the team as former Eastbourne and Hastings star Jock Grierson was signed up in place of Genz who was loaned out to second division Yarmouth.

Apart from one match, the New Cross team now remained intact for nine matches. Without illness or injury, they were free to show what they could do and, of those nine matches, they won seven, including four away, culminating in a massive 63-21 win over

Norwich, putting them top of the Coronation Cup table. With Grierson in for Genz there was no weak link in the team and even Longley was putting up much better performances than he had done in the previous year or two.

Towards the middle of May, Harding announced that he was fit to return, as a result of which the Ministry of Labour, backed by the SRA, refused to grant an extension to Nygren's work permit. Nygren had been instrumental in New Cross's revival, chalking up double-figure scores in six of the 11 fixtures he had ridden in, and averaging 10.40. Mockford appealed once again to the Control Board to urge the Ministry of Labour to allow Nygren to stay, otherwise, he said, New Cross would be too weak to hold its own in the National League and that with a team too weak to put up a reasonable showing in the league the crowds would stay away.

Even without the prospect of a weaker team, Mockford was already concerned that he was losing too much money and argued with his fellow promoters that start and bonus points money for the riders should be cut, but the SRA naturally would not agree to this. Mockford explained that the crowds were just not coming in the same numbers as they had been five or six years previously and that he was now averaging just about 5,000 per meeting instead of the five-figure crowds that were common in the late 1940s.

In the end, Mockford's exasperation with the Control Board and the S.R.A over both Nygren and pay rates reached breaking point and he was losing so much money that he felt he had no alternative but to announce the closure of New Cross Speedway. He cited as reasons for this: the competition from television; the crippling level of entertainment tax; the lack of traveling facilities; the extraordinarily wet summer; the shortage of spending money which had been exacerbated by the Coronation celebrations, and the fact that he could not provide his spectators with the team he felt was necessary to give proper entertainment.

And so, in the season that Fred Mockford should have been celebrating twenty-five years in speedway with Crystal Palace and New Cross, he packed it all in, turning his back on the sport he had loved and in which he had played such a key part for a quarter of a century. Just days after the closure was announced, the Control Board put out a notice saying that agreement had been reached on cutting riders' pay rates. Start money was reduced from 35s to 30s and second-half prize money was also cut. It was reckoned that promoters would save roughly £65 per meeting.

1953 – Coronation Cup

11 April	A	Belle Vue	L	34-50
15 April	H	Harringay	W	56-28
18 April	A	Norwich	W	47-37
20 April	A	Wimbledon	L	40-44
22 April	H	Wembley	W	49-35
29 April	H	Belle Vue	W	47-37
2 May	A	Bradford	W	43-41

5 May	A	West Ham	W	44-40
6 May	H	Norwich	W	63-21
13 May	H	Birmingham	W	43-40
15 May	A	Bristol	D	41.5-41.5
20 May	H	Wimbledon	W	44-40
27 May	H	Bristol	L	41-43
30 May	A	Birmingham	L	39-45
3 June	H	West Ham	L	41-42
10 June	H	Bradford	D	42-42

P16 W9 D2 L5

For 714.5 points; Against 546.5 points

New Cross withdrew from cup before completion

1953 – London Cup

First round

Bye

Semi-final

| 12 June | A | Harringay | L | 44-64 |

Second leg not ridden. Harringay awarded tie

1953 – Coronation Cup Averages

Rider	M	R	Pts	BP	T	CMA	FM	PM
Olle Nygren	10	40	94	10	104	10.40	0	1
Eric French	16	64	132	10	142	8.86	1	1
Bert Roger	15	56	123	1	124	8.86	1	0
Cyril Roger	16	62	117	10	127	8.19	0	1
Merv Harding	7	28	33	10	43	6.14	0	0
Bill Longley	16	58	68.5	17	85.5	5.90	0	1
Jock Grierson	15	38	47	5	52	5.47	0	0
Bob Roger	16	59	66	9	75	5.08	0	0
Frank Lawrence	15	41	24	7	31	3.02	0	0

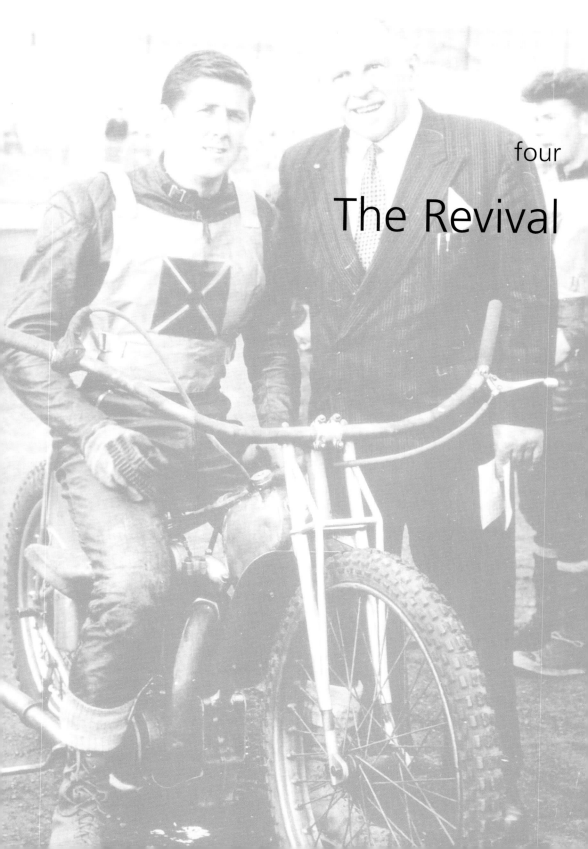

four

The Revival

1959

Following a period of decline in the 1950s precipitated by New Cross's closure, the year 1959 saw the beginnings of the sport's revival as a number of defunct tracks in the North and Midlands reopened. As well as these, there was one defunct track reopened in London by former rider Phil 'Tiger' Hart and Johnnie Hoskins. Hoskins, one of the greatest showmen the sport had ever seen, had been promoting speedway in Australia and Britain since 1923 and had been the manager of Wembley, West Ham and Newcastle amongst others. In his days as manager of West Ham in the 1930s he had had a particular rivalry with Fred Mockford at New Cross. To Mockford and the New Cross supporters, Hoskins had always been known as the Bishop of Barking Creek. The track Hoskins and Hart reopened was New Cross.

At 7.45 p.m. on 19 August, the moment all South East London had been waiting six years for finally arrived, as the track officials and riders marched out to the familiar strains of *Marching Along Together*. Those spectators who had bought a programme turned to the first page to see a message from Johnnie Hoskins, which began: 'Hello London. Long time no see.'

The match itself took the form of a challenge between a makeshift New Cross team, made up of riders from other clubs, and Wimbledon. Captain for the day was Cyril Roger, while one of the other members of the team was Ronnie Genz.

In all, eight meetings were held in 1959 – on the new track now slightly lengthened to 278 yards – in the form of challenge matches and individual meetings. Cyril Roger captained the team in all the matches. Other regulars included Belle Vue's Peter Craven, Wimbledon's Peter Moore and Coventry's Ron Mountford. In the final programme, Hoskins promised that New Cross would be back again next Easter, though he gave no promise about what sort of racing would be seen there.

NEW CROSS

SPEEDWAY

WEDNESDAY, AUGUST 19, 1959

Commencing 7.45 p.m.

NEW CROSS RANGERS v WIMBLEDON

47   *43*

OFFICIAL PROGRAMME – – – **6**D.

Programme cover for 19 August 1959, the first meeting of New Cross's revival.

1960

It was, of course, Hoskins's ambition and intention to bring New Cross back to the top flight and so, over the winter, he worked hard on getting a team together that would be good enough to enter the National League. Tiger Hart left the promotion to open Birmingham and Hoskins brought in a new partner, Stan Hinckley.

Hoskins' first big signing was former Wembley and Harringay's world no.2, the thirty-seven-year-old Split Waterman, who had retired midway through the 1958 season. At the same time as his appointment was announced, the New Cross management put out a statement saying: 'Moves towards building a strong team for entry to the National League are well under way. If all goes according to plan, the Rangers team will include Waterman, Maury Dunn, Rune Sormander, Leo McAuliffe, Tommy Sweetman and former Wembley rider, Jimmy Gooch.' Hoskins was also after the same man whose loss had been one of the causes of their closure in 1953, Olle Nygren. Nygren, however, quickly ruled himself out as he said he was unable to commit to a full season due to business commitments and continental race bookings.

With the news that New Cross were returning, several former Rangers were touted as possibilities for the starting line-up, including Cyril and Bert Roger, Ray Moore and Bill Longley. Ron Johnson was also said to be returning from Australia to look for a coaching or managerial position with his old club.

On 6 February, Hoskins, in conjunction with the supporters' club, organised a dance for the supporters and prospective riders. Held at the Central Baths, Bermondsey, it was said to be the most successful speedway dance since speedway's halcyon days of the late 1940s. Over forty riders turned up including Waterman, Longley, Genz, McAuliffe, Sweetman, Stan Stevens, Peter Sampson, Vic White, Bobby Croombs and the current world champion, Ronnie Moore. During the evening it was announced that former

Leo McAuliffe rode for New Cross in 1960 and 1961.

Wembley star Eric Williams had agreed to return from his home in New Zealand to ride for the Rangers in 1960.

As the season approached, Hoskins announced one more signing, that of Swede Arne Carlsson. With riders of the calibre of Waterman, Williams, Carlsson, McAuliffe and Gooch signed up as definite starters, New Cross applied for and were granted a place in the National League. It was not a strong team, but it was good enough.

Before the season started, a practice meeting was held. Riders at the practice included Ray Moore, McAuliffe, Sweetman, Croombs and Reg Luckhurst. Also present as observers were Waterman and Cyril Roger, who was hobbling around on crutches and looking very unlikely to make any line-up let alone the New Cross team. At the meeting, Croombs announced that he had turned down the offer of a contract with Bristol to ride for New Cross.

The opening meeting took place on 6 April. It was an individual trophy meeting called the South London Cup and was won by Wimbledon's Ronnie Moore. His namesake, Ray Moore, still hoping for a place in the new Rangers line-up, had three point-less rides before retiring for the night. The best placed of the New Cross team was Waterman who finished in fifth place with 10 points.

New Cross's new team for the new era had its first outing the following week in a challenge match against Norwich. After months of speculation and team building the team that finally made that first line-up was Waterman, Gooch, Carlsson, Croombs, Williams and McAuliffe, with Luckhurst and Derek Timms at reserve. At that opening meeting it was the man on the red bike who captured the hearts of this new generation of New Cross supporters. Arne Carlsson gave a storming display of racing, winning his first four races the hard way, coming from the back each time. His do-or-die style of racing had the fans leaping to their feet with excitement every time he rode. As well as being content with his new crowd pleaser, Hoskins was also very gratified at the riding of his captain, Split Waterman, as he turned in a paid maximum. Even better was the fact that he and his partner Gooch scored a 5-1 in their three races together. The 66-24 victory over Norwich was a good beginning and showed promise of great things to come.

Having now arrived from Australia, former New Cross captain and hero Ron Johnson was in the crowd for this meeting. Afterwards he announced his intention of getting back into the saddle and renewing his racing career with the Rangers. There were some who applauded his courage, but there were many more voices who thought this course of action very unwise, especially in view of the bad time he had had towards the end of his career and the fact that he had celebrated his fifty-third birthday in February. Hoskins' view was that if he got the okay from the Control Board he would let him ride as he was still a big name in New Cross. Because of his age, the Control Board sent Johnson to a medical examiner to pass judgment on his fitness, but Johnson himself said he felt far fitter now than he had when he was last in England as a rider.

New Cross did not fare so well in their first away encounter, going down 35-54 at Ipswich. But once again it was Carlsson who made everyone sit up and take notice as he scorched to 15 points from five rides.

The first official fixture was a Britannia Shield match away at Swindon. The Britannia Shield was a new competition which had been introduced in 1957 in an attempt to save money by being run on a regional basis, with a southern section and a northern section. The winners of each section met in the final to decide the destiny of the shield. Once again Carlsson was the only New Cross rider to show any sort of fight as the Rangers were murdered 62-28.

After their brilliant start in the challenge match against Norwich, the Rangers' season went from bad to worse and they lost the first six of their official Britannia Shield fixtures, including two at home. Towards the end of this period, Carlsson's form dropped alarmingly. He returned to Sweden after scoring just two points in five rides against Swindon on 27 April, where he was taken ill. Effectively, New Cross were down to just two riders, Waterman and Williams, who could score any points at all. The rest were struggling both at home and away.

The Britannia Shield meeting on 11 May at home to Norwich turned out to be New Cross's first official win. The rest of the team at last managed to get amongst the points. In fact, Gooch was top scorer with 11. With the usual good performances from Williams and Waterman and with McAuliffe, Croombs, Timms and Luckhurst all managing to defeat their Norwich counterparts, it was a different Rangers team as they beat the Stars 48-42.

Meanwhile, Johnson had been given the go-ahead to race again and was currently appearing in second halves, but he was just a pale shadow of the rider that had once been British Individual Champion and Australian Test captain as he struggled to hold his own with even the rawest of novices. He did, however, take his place as captain of the New Cross Colts team that travelled to Edinburgh and won 40-32 against the home side. Others in the team were Croombs, Luckhurst, Timms, Sweetman, Jimmy Chalkley and Harold Want. He scored a total of three points, and those who saw him score them say they will never forget it as it was a real flashback to the Johnson of old. All his points came from one race win when he shot out of the gate and then actually slowed down, holding up the opposition to allow his partner to come through into second place. Once he had assured himself that they were on course for a 5-1, he tore off again, winning the race with ease. It was a real flash of the vintage Johnson. As a result of this, Hoskins sent Johnson up to his son Ian's promotion at Edinburgh to see if some outings in the Provincial League could restore his confidence and form. In all he rode in six matches for Edinburgh, managing just one point and one bonus point. Former Edinburgh rider, Bert Harkins, who saw Johnson said that what amazed him was that when the lines went up, 'Johnson was out of the gate like lightning; his reactions were still razor sharp but the problem was that he could not hold on to the bike for a whole race'. Dennis Wallace, an Edinburgh supporter, saw these six matches and said:

It was probably just as well that Ian Hoskins pulled the plug on this last chapter in his career. There was a sense of horror every time he took to the track because his arms were clearly not strong enough to hold on to the machine properly and he was a dreadful accident just waiting to happen. I think he frightened the other riders in the race as much as the spectators although you had to admire his guts for giving it a go if not his common sense!

It was a sad end for the man who had been associated with the club for thirty-two years and the captain and backbone for over twenty.

In spite of the home win over Norwich, it was obvious that New Cross needed strengthening, especially in view of the fact that Carlsson had now gone for good. At first the Control Board agreed that New Cross could sign up a replacement Swede in either Rune Sormander or Olle Nygren, but before Hoskins could talk to either of them, Ronnie Greene, the Wimbledon promoter, told him that he would allow former World Champion and Dons' asset Barry Briggs to join the Rangers on loan for the rest of the season. Hoskins cabled Briggs, who was still in New Zealand, immediately, offering him a place in the New Cross team. Briggs accepted and returned in time for the home National League match against Ipswich on 1 June.

Having arrived without his bike, Briggs was mounted on the track spare. In his first race he had plug trouble, which restricted him to third place, and in his second ride the throttle jammed open and he careered into the safety fence, crashing right under it and finishing up on the greyhound track, fortunately without injury.

His first major contribution to the side came on 6 June in New Cross's last Britannia Shield match. Back on his old stamping ground at Wimbledon, Briggs turned in a confident performance, scoring 10 points, though he was still eclipsed by Williams who managed 13 paid 15. Neither score was good enough to prevent New Cross suffering another heavy defeat, going down 31–56.

Thanks to some strong support from Waterman and McAuliffe, Williams's 15-point maximum and Briggs's 12 points were enough to break the long run of defeats in their next National League match as they scored a convincing 53–37 win over Leicester.

Briggs was now settling into the role Hoskins had hoped for and was becoming a regular double-points man. With Williams also matching him meeting for meeting, New Cross had two riders who were able to take on the best in the league. The problem was the rest were very patchy. Waterman had some good meetings, but there were others where he could hardly score anything. McAuliffe and Gooch also had their ups and downs. The problem was it was very rare for the three to have a good meeting at the same time. Nevertheless, with the consistently good riding from Williams and Briggs, it usually made for a close match. The real problem was in the sixth team place. Hoskins tried out Sweetman, Croombs and Timms, but none of them were really up to second-string standard and, although they could hold their own with the opposition's reserves, this one step up was proving a problem for the team.

However, by the end of June, New Cross had got over the 'Cinderella' image they had acquired at the start of the season and were generally winning at home, while even away they were now putting in some good performances. On 16 June they came within an ace of pulling off their first away victory, losing by just two points at Oxford, 44–46. Then on 1 July, they finally made it with a 49–41 victory away at Leicester, with Briggs scoring his first full maximum of the season.

However, the inconsistency of the rest of the team meant this was New Cross's only away victory all year and, when Williams left early to return home to New Zealand because of domestic problems, it was the end of their season as they lost their last five matches, including one at home to Norwich by the massive score of 29–61. Although all five matches were lost, Briggs was getting better and better and finished with a flourish, scoring two full maximums, away at Wimbledon and Norwich.

New Cross had started the year with very much an unknown team. Although top riders in their time, Waterman and Williams had come out of retirement and Hoskins was taking a bit of a gamble on their being able to recapture their old form. The gamble paid off handsomely with Williams, who rode as well as at any time in his career, but

Waterman did not quite hit the big time again. Apart from Gooch, the rest of the team were mostly young, up-and-coming riders who had been making their name in the Southern Area League. McAuliffe turned out to be easily the best of the bunch, and turned in some good performances but was inconsistent.

On an individual level, both Briggs and Williams qualified for the World Championship final, although Williams had to leave before the final took place. Briggs finished in sixth place with nine points. Briggs was also chosen to contest the British Match Race Championship, but lost 2-0 to Ove Fundin at New Cross and then 2-0 at Norwich.

Hoskins summed up the season by saying: 'My team would be okay if only they'd stop losing.' But then added, in a more serious way: 'We started off with no riders at all and entered the league wondering just where the team was coming from… In the end our team have done better than we ever thought possible and at least we can start 1961 much better off than this year.' It had been a gamble bringing New Cross back from the dead, but one that had paid off.

Over the winter, Hinkley left the promotion and Hoskins joined up with two new co-promoters: Nobby Attwill and former West Ham rider Ken Brett.

1960 – National League

21 May	A	Coventry	L	27-63
1 June	H	Ipswich	L	44-45
4 June	A	Belle Vue	L	33-57
8 June	H	Leicester	W	53-37
15 June	H	Southampton	W	50-37
16 June	A	Oxford	L	44-46
22 June	H	Coventry	W	49-40
1 July	A	Leicester	W	53-37
13 July	H	Wimbledon	W	47-43
14 July	A	Ipswich	L	36-55
3 August	H	Belle Vue	D	45-45
10 August	H	Oxford	W	47-42
17 August	H	Swindon	W	53-33
27 August	A	Norwich	L	29-61
30 August	A	Southampton	L	35-55
31 August	H	Norwich	L	42-47
5 September	A	Wimbledon	L	42-48
24 September	A	Swindon	L	43-47

P18 W7 D1 L10

For 770 points; Against 840 points

Finished 8th (out of 10)

Barry Briggs (left) New Cross's top rider in 1960, with Johnnie Hoskins.

1960 – National Trophy

First round

25 June	A	Norwich	L	41–67
29 June	H	Norwich	W	61–47

Lost 102–114 on aggregate

1960 – Britannia Shield

23 April	A	Swindon	L	28–62
26 April	A	Southampton	L	24–66
27 April	H	Swindon	L	35–55
4 May	H	Southampton	L	36–54
7 May	A	Norwich	L	24–56
11 May	H	Norwich	W	48–42
18 May	H	Wimbledon	L	28–62
6 June	A	Wimbledon	L	31–56

P8 W1 D0 L7

For 254 points; Against 453 points
Finished 5th (out of 5)

1960 – National League Averages

Rider	M	R	Pts	BP	T	CMA	FM	PM
Barry Briggs	15	75	178	6	184	9.81	3	1
Eric Williams	12	63	143	5	148	9.40	2	0
Split Waterman	17	72	113	14	127	7.06	1	0
Leo McAuliffe	17	70	96	12	118	6.74	0	0
Jimmy Gooch	17	70	71	17	88	5.03	0	0
Bobby Croombs	15	42	35	7	42	4.00	0	0
Derek Timms	14	35	26	5	31	3.54	0	0
Tommy Sweetman	17	43	30	6	36	3.35	0	0

1961

Johnnie Hoskins had made his reputation in speedway as its greatest showman. He was continually thinking up new ways to gain publicity and bring in the crowds. The start of the 1961 season was no exception as he announced that he was looking for young riders and was offering novices rides in the second half at New Cross. He made three provisos for any youngster wishing to apply. The first was that they had to be under nineteen years of age and the second was that they had to have their own bike and equipment. But it was the third condition that made the headlines which even the national Press picked up: he stipulated that before he allowed any novice a ride at New Cross they had to sign a contract which guaranteed they would not get married for twelve months. Hoskins justified this by saying: 'Single boys are more popular with the fans. The single girls like to think they've got a chance to land one for a husband.'

After encouraging youngsters to apply for a spin at New Cross, Hoskins then promptly did away with practice meetings before the season. He said they served no purpose and did the motors and riders no good. The first time the riders saw the track, therefore, was at the opening meeting on 31 March, a London Cup first-leg tie against Wimbledon. It was a very depleted Rangers team that turned out for this first match. Williams had not yet returned from New Zealand and Hoskins had so far been unable to come to terms with Briggs for the new season. During the winter, Hoskins had been offered the chance of signing up old Rangers stalwart Cyril Roger, as Norwich had placed him on the transfer market, but New Cross did not feel he was worth the asking fee of £150, so he moved to Southampton instead. Timms left, having been transferred to Cradley Heath. Luckhurst was recalled from Edinburgh, where he had spent most of the 1960 season on loan, to take his place while a new

Swede, Bengt Brannefors, had been signed up. But without Briggs and Williams, the Rangers took a real hammering, losing 39–68.

Shortly after this match, Hoskins announced that he had been unsuccessful in trying to lure Briggs back and had turned his attention to South African rider Doug Davies. Davies had last ridden in England during 1955 as a member of the Birmingham side and had qualified for the World Championship final in that year. Since then he had been racing in South Africa and was the country's no.1. He readily agreed to make a comeback to England to ride for the Rangers.

New Cross faced their first big challenge on 14 April when they were due to meet Leicester away in the first round of the newly instituted Knock Out Cup. This was to be run like Football's FA Cup on a single-match basis rather than the normal home

Eric Williams rode for New Cross in 1960 and 1961.

The 1961 New Cross team. From left to right: Doug Davies, Reg Luckhurst, Nobby Atwill (co-promoter), Split Waterman (captain, on bike), Johnnie Fitzpatrick, Leo McAuliffe, Ken Brett (co-promoter), Jimmy Gooch, Eric Williams, Johnnie Hoskins (co-promoter and manager).

and away legs. Teams for National League and Knock Out Cup matches had been reduced to seven with the racing format also reduced to 13 heats in a bid to save money.

Williams and Davies had still not arrived and, in addition, Sweetman had been transferred to Wolverhampton. So the team that took part in this fixture consisted of Waterman, Gooch, McAuliffe, Croombs, Luckhurst, Brannefors and a newcomer to the side, Johnnie Fitzpatrick. To most pundits this looked like the team that was going to finish bottom of the National League. But there was a big surprise in store as the Rangers rode brilliantly to beat their opponents on their own track. Both Brannefors and Gooch score paid maximums, while McAuliffe and Croombs added eight and seven points respectively. There was now much more hope amongst the loyal fans that when Williams and Davies arrived, they would have a team to match anyone in the league.

However, with Williams and Davies still missing, New Cross began their league campaign with home and away matches against the favourites for the title, Southampton. Ironically, Southampton included in their team both Briggs and Roger who were instrumental in the Saints' two big wins over the Rangers: 56-22 at Southampton and 45-31 at home.

With still no sign of Williams or Davies, the Rangers took on Belle Vue at home. There was an even bigger blow to the Rangers' chances as Gooch was suffering from a leg injury and had been ordered by his doctor not to ride and Brannefors cabled Hoskins just before the meeting to say he would be unable to get to England in time. Because of this, Gooch decided to ignore his medical advice and turn out for his team. He went to the track to get in a few practice laps, but had to give it up as his leg was too painful. However, he then had the bright idea of raising his saddle and handlebars three inches so that he wouldn't have to bend his leg. He said it felt like riding a penny-farthing bicycle. The main thing was that it worked, and it was a good job it did as he was able to put in an outstanding performance, rattling off nine points, one win and three second places. In addition to Gooch's heroics, for the first time in the season, Waterman put up the sort of display everyone knew he was capable of, scoring ten paid eleven. Even so, the scores were level going into the last heat, but a 5-1 from McAuliffe and Waterman gave the home side their first victory in four matches. After the match, Hoskins told supporters that, because of his unreliability, the services of Brannefors had been dispensed with.

Williams returned in time for the next home meeting, a London v. The Rest challenge match, only to find that his bike had been stolen from his garage during his absence. Riding on the track spare, he managed just three third places in London's 40-38 victory.

Finally, the moment all New Cross fans had been waiting for came on 17 May as both Williams and Davies lined up for the Rangers in the home league match against Oxford. The result was a team that could now hold its own with anyone and scored a 44-34 victory.

New Cross's relief was short-lived, however, as they promptly lost their next match, 46-32, away at Coventry. But far worse was to follow as, on 22 May they were slaughtered by a rampant Wimbledon team to the tune of 60-18. Fortunately, the team bounced back in the next home fixture, defeating Ipswich 55-23. It was a bit of a false dawn, however, as the Rangers then lost their next four league matches. In the middle of this poor run in the league, New Cross took on Belle Vue in the first round of the National Trophy. They fared no better here, going down 74-92 on aggregate.

New Cross broke their bad run in the league with a 44-33 victory over Swindon on 14 June and then finished the league season with three more wins and two losses. Perhaps the main reason for this better run at the end of the league season was the form of their captain, Split Waterman. In the early 1950s, Waterman had been one of the best riders in the world, twice finishing runner-up in the World Championship and for a short time holding the British Match Race title.

Although still just about heat-leader class following his return to racing in 1960, he was nothing like the rider he had once been. Suddenly, however, in the middle of 1961 the old Waterman reappeared. On 28 June, in a league match against Norwich, he beat the current world champion, Ove Fundin, twice. New Cross was one of Fundin's favourite tracks, he was track record holder at 57 seconds and was very rarely beaten there. Not only did Waterman beat him twice in the match on his way to a paid maximum, but he also beat him in the second half. The following week, Waterman won the New Cross qualifying round of the World Championship, beating the likes of Nigel Boocock, Bob Andrews and Ken McKinlay in the process. A full maximum against Coventry came next and then he top-scored for the winning England team in the World Team Championship qualifying round with 13 points. For New Cross fans, it was a real privilege to see Waterman recapture the form that had made him one of the greatest riders of all times, albeit for just a short period.

Unfortunately for their chances of doing better in the league, Waterman's resurgence came a bit too late as the league season finished early and the second half of the season was mostly taken up with challenge matches and individual trophies. In the end, New Cross finished 1961 in the same position as they had finished 1960, eighth out of ten.

None of the New Cross riders qualified for the World Championship final; Davies got the nearest, qualifying for the British Final, where he scored five points to come thirteenth.

At the end of the season, Hoskins wrote in his programme notes:

We have not reached the heights in the League, so our crowds were not as large as we should have liked… however, folks, we have had lots of really good racing. Every meeting has been first-class… next season perhaps we shall do ever so much better. So now it's cheerio from all the riders and may we meet again around the speedway next Easter.

But Hoskins and his riders never did meet the fans at Easter 1962. After the season finished, Hoskins split with Atwill and Brett and was left in sole charge of New Cross. However, the GRA, who owned the stadium, received a better offer to run stock cars on the track and they told Hoskins that he could no longer promote speedway at the stadium. The end, when it finally came in February was a shock to everyone, not least the secretary of the Supporters' Club who only found out about the closure when he read it in the evening paper.

It now looked as if speedway racing was finished for ever at the Frying Pan, but it wasn't quite the end.

1961 – National League

18 April	A	Southampton	L	22-56
19 April	H	Southampton	L	31-45
27 April	A	Oxford	L	30-48
3 May	H	Belle Vue	W	41-37
5 May	A	Leicester	L	32-46
17 May	H	Oxford	W	44-34
20 May	A	Coventry	L	32-46
24 May	H	Ipswich	W	55-23
27 May	A	Norwich	L	23-55

31 May	H	Wimbledon	L	34-44
1 June	A	Ipswich	L	27-51
12 June	A	Wimbledon	L	18-60
14 June	H	Swindon	W	44-33
28 June	H	Norwich	W	51-27
19 July	H	Coventry	W	47-31
22 July	A	Belle Vue	L	17-60
29 July	A	Swindon	L	24-54
9 August	H	Leicester	W	54-24

P18 W7 D0 L11
For 626 points; Against 774 points
Finished 8th (out of 10)

1961 – National Trophy

First round

7 June	H	Belle Vue	W	46-37
10 June	A	Belle Vue	L	28-55

Lost 74-92 on aggregate

1961 – Knock-Out Cup

First round

14 April	A	Leicester	W	43-35

Second round

26 April	H	Wimbledon	L	31-47

London Cup

31 March	H	Wimbledon	L	39-68
31 March	A	Wimbledon	L	30-78

Lost on aggregate 69-146

1961 – National League Averages

Rider	M	R	Pts	BP	T	CMA	FM	PM
Split Waterman	17	72	133	14	147	8.17	1	1
Doug Davies	13	53	80	13	93	7.02	0	2
Eric Williams	13	52	82	5	87	6.69	0	0
Leo McAuliffe	18	73	99	19	118	6.47	0	0
Jimmy Gooch	17	64	96	6	102	6.38	0	2
Reg Luckhurst	18	71	77	11	88	4.96	0	0
Johnnie Fitzpatrick	13	35	34	5	39	4.46	0	0
Bobby Croombs	11	32	22	8	30	3.75	0	0

1963

In early 1963 there was a flurry of activity in South East London as two experienced promoters and former riders, Wally Mawdsley and Pete Lansdale, entered into discussions with the GRA to see if it would be possible to stage speedway racing once again on the New Cross circuit. On 22 February the pair held a public meeting at the Drill Hall in Jamaica Road, to announce their plans for the coming season.

At this meeting, Mawdsley and Lansdale explained that their negotiations had proved successful and they had entered the new Rangers into the Provincial League, the first time that New Cross had not been in the senior tier of racing. However, they felt the racing would be as exciting as it had always been and by entering the 'second division' costs would be lower, which would benefit both the promoters and supporters alike. Vic Gooden was named as the team manager and former Walthamstow and Rayleigh rider Reg Reeves as captain. Reeves had actually ridden as a junior in second halves at New Cross as far back as 1948. Others included in the team were Bobby Dugard, Geoff Penniket, Tony Marren and Reg Reeves's son, Eddie. Apart from the new captain, all the riders named were youngsters who it was hoped would improve with experience. However, the surprise name was left until last and the room caught its collective breath as the two promoters announced they had signed up former New Cross no.1, Bert Roger.

Over the next month extensive work took place at the stadium as they had to rip up the stock-car base, resurface the track and erect a new safety fence. The work went ahead on schedule and as the day for the opening meeting approached, all was well down at the Old Kent Road, except for one thing. no one had heard from Bert Roger since before Christmas.

Although Roger's name actually made it on to the Hackney programme for New Cross's first match of the season, an away challenge match held on 10 April, he never

RANGERS v. POOLE
(PROVINCIAL LEAGUE)
FRIDAY, AUGUST 2, 1963
OFFICIAL PROGRAMME 9d.

Programme cover for the last
meeting ever staged at the
Frying Pan, 2 August, 1963.

did make it back into the team, which consisted of the two Reeves, Dugard, Penniket and three new signings, Stan Stevens, Des Lukehurst and the forty-one-year-old veteran Jimmy Squibb. It was an exciting close encounter as the Rangers drew 38-38 with Squibb scoring 11 points.

Two days later, New Cross had their first home fixture, a Southern League clash with Hackney, which they won 45-33. It was a good start to the season, which continued into May, as the Rangers won their first four matches, including a first-round Knock Out Cup victory over St Austell and an away win at Rayleigh. Squibb, in particular, made a sensational start to the season as he followed up his 11 points at Hackney with three maximums, as well as taking the Silver Sash title from Exeter's Len Silver on 22 April.

The winning run came to an end on 6 May when they lost 53-25 away at Exeter, where Squibb also lost his Silver Sash title to the man he had beaten in the first place, Len Silver. They finished up their Southern League fixtures with two home wins and two away losses, Squibb added two more maximums in the two home matches and another in the away loss at Hackney. In the end, the Rangers finished the league in third place behind Poole and Exeter.

Incredibly, rumours began to circulate that Ron Johnson wanted to try another comeback for his old team and Mawdsley and Lansdale arranged for living accommodation for him. On 14 May, he once again took to the track and defeated Phil Bishop 2-1 in a second-half match race series. However, Johnson, wisely in the opinion of many, decided not to pursue the idea of a full-time return and his racing career finally came to an end after having been with the Crystal Palace/New Cross set-up from their first season in 1928 to their last in 1963 – a span of thirty-five years.

New Cross opened their Provincial League season on 21 May with a convincing 44-34 win over Newcastle. Once again, Squibb scored a maximum. He had now completed five home fixtures without losing a race. He was receiving good backing from heat leaders Reg Reeves and Bob Dugard with Stan Stevens proving to be a useful second string.

Although New Cross's Provincial League campaign got off to a good start with their win over Newcastle, their chances of continued success were dealt a severe blow on 22 May in a Southern League match at Poole as captain Reg Reeves was badly injured in a crash. The following night, without him, New Cross lost heavily at Middlesbrough, 27-51. Squibb scored over half the team's points with 14.

Reg Reeves's injury proved more serious than at first thought and without him the Rangers began to struggle. New Cross were operating with three heat leaders, Squibb, Reeves and Dugard, with quite a gap before the top second string. Stevens was promoted to heat leader but he was not really up to that standard. Squibb was still carrying all before him and Dugard was also invariably in the points, but the tail was far too long. With no real third-heat leader and with no strong second string to take Stevens's place, the team lost their next five matches.

As the season wore on and there was no sign of Reeves's return, New Cross looked destined for a final position somewhere near the bottom of the table. Following the run of five losses, the team lost a further seven out of nine official matches, including a 42-54 defeat at the hands of Hackney in the Knock Out Cup.

The last match in the sequence came on 5 August, when the Rangers were comprehensively thrashed at Poole, 51-27. Sadly, this was the last match ever ridden by a team wearing the familiar orange and black of New Cross as Mawdsley and Lansdale reluctantly decided they had no option but to pull the plug and prevent themselves 'running into the ground', as Mawdsley put it.

Four thousand people had attended the first meeting of the season back on Good Friday, but for various reasons, those numbers had fallen dramatically. Two in particular were advanced, firstly the poor record of the team after Reeves's accident. The Rangers had lost 12 out of 16 Provincial League fixtures, including four at home. The second was that New Cross supporters were used to seeing only the world's best riders and good as Squibb and Reeves were, they were 'second division' riders and were just not in the same class as Tom Farndon, Ron Johnson, George Newton, Jack Milne, Cyril Roger, Barry Briggs or Split Waterman.

The last time speedway was seen at the Old Kent Road track itself was on 2 April 1962, a Provincial League match against Poole, which New Cross lost 37-41. The very last race ever seen there was the Late Night Rangers' Stakes final, which was won by Stan Stevens from Poole's Tony Lewis and Geoff Mudge, with Jimmy Squibb in last place, who thus became the last rider ever to cross the line at the Frying Pan.

1963 – Provincial League

21 May	H	Newcastle	W	44-34
23 May	A	Middlesbrough	L	27-51
28 May	H	Sheffield	W	42-35
3 June	A	Exeter	L	30-48
3 June	A	St Austell	L	25-53
4 June	H	St Austell	L	38-39
18 June	H	Wolverhampton	L	35-43
29 June	A	Stoke	L	29-48
2 July	H	Middlesbrough	W	41-36
9 July	H	Stoke	L	35-43
15 July	A	Newcastle	L	31-47
16 July	H	Long Eaton	W	44-32
20 July	A	Cradley Heath	L	34-44
26 July	A	Wolverhampton	L	35-43
2 August	H	Poole	L	37-41
5 August	A	Poole	L	27-51

P16 W4 D0 L12

For 554 points; Against 688 points
Withdrew from league before completion.

1963 – Knock Out Cup

First round

30 April	H	St Austell	W	58-37

Second round

10 July	A	Hackney	L	42-54

1963 – Southern League

12 April	H	Hackney	W	45–33
23 April	H	Exeter	W	45–32
4 May	A	Rayleigh	W	43–35
6 May	A	Exeter	L	25–53
7 May	H	Poole	W	40–38
14 May	H	Rayleigh	W	40–36
15 May	A	Hackney	L	38–40
22 May	A	Poole	L	31–47

P8 W5 D0 L3

For 297; Against 316

Finished 3rd (out of 5)

1963 – Provincial League Averages

Rider	M	R	Pts	BP	T	CMA	FM	PM
Jimmy Squibb	16	71	173	2	175	9.86	2	1
Bob Dugard	15	63	104	10	114	7.24	1	0
John Dugard	9	37	45	10	55	5.95	0	0
Stan Stevens	16	68	93	7	100	5.88	0	0
Geoff Penniket	16	59	70	11	81	5.49	0	0
Des Lukehurst	9	31	19	8	27	3.48	0	0
Eddie Reeves	14	37	13	6	19	2.05	0	0
Terry Stone	7	22	8	1	9	1.64	0	0

Appendix

Four-Lap Clutch-Start Track Record

262 Yard Track (1934–1953)

18 April 1934	63.0	Tom Farndon
20 June 1934	61.4	Tom Farndon
25 July 1934	60.8	Ron Johnson
17 April 1935	60.6	Jack Parker
1 May 1935	60.4	Tom Farndon
22 May 1935	59.6	Tom Farndon★
10 July 1935	58.4	Tom Farndon
20 March 1938	58.0	George Newton
7 June 1939	58.0	Arthur Atkinson
2 June 1948	57.8	Ron Johnson
3 May 1950	57.4	Eric French
5 July 1950	57.0	Bert Roger
6 June 1951	56.6	Cyril Roger
3 October 1951	56.0	Cyril Roger

278 Yard Track (1959–1963)

19 August 1959	58.0	Ronnie Moore
29 June 1960	57.6	Ove Fundin
27 July 1960	57.0	Ove Fundin

★ This was the first time that a rider had completed four laps of a speedway track under one minute from a clutch start anywhere in the country.